W9-AZB-531

ELEVEN OUT OF TEN

ELEVEN OUT OF TEN

The Life and Work of
DAVID
PECAUT

Helen Burstyn

DUNDURN
TORONTO

Copyright © Helen Burstyn, 2012

All rights reserved. No part of this publication may be reproduced, stored in a retrieval system, or transmitted in any form or by any means, electronic, mechanical, photocopying, recording, or otherwise (except for brief passages for purposes of review) without the prior permission of Dundurn Press. Permission to photocopy should be requested from Access Copyright.

Project Editor: Shannon Whibbs
Copy Editor: Andrea Waters
Design: Courtney Horner
Printer: Trigraphik LBF

Library and Archives Canada Cataloguing in Publication

Burstyn, Helen
    Eleven out of ten : the life and work of David Pecaut / by Helen Burstyn.

Includes index.
Issued also in electronic formats.
ISBN 978-1-4597-0792-4

    1. Pecaut, David, 1955-2009. 2. Civic leaders--Ontario--Toronto--
Biography. 3. Volunteers--Ontario--Toronto--Biography. 4. Toronto (Ont.)--
Social life and customs--Anecdotes. 5. Toronto (Ont.)--Biography. I. Title.

FC3097.26.P43B87 2012   971.3'54104092   C2012-904637-X

1 2 3 4 5   16 15 14 13 12

We acknowledge the support of the **Canada Council for the Arts** and the **Ontario Arts Council** for our publishing program. We also acknowledge the financial support of the **Government of Canada** through the **Canada Book Fund** and **Livres Canada Books**, and the **Government of Ontario** through the **Ontario Book Publishing Tax Credit** and the **Ontario Media Development Corporation**.

Care has been taken to trace the ownership of copyright material used in this book. The author and the publisher welcome any information enabling them to rectify any references or credits in subsequent editions.

J. Kirk Howard, President

Printed and bound in Canada.
www.dundurn.com

Visit us at
Dundurn.com
Definingcanada.ca
@dundurnpress
Facebook.com/dundurnpress

Dundurn	Gazelle Book Services Limited	Dundurn
3 Church Street, Suite 500	White Cross Mills	2250 Military Road
Toronto, Ontario, Canada	High Town, Lancaster, England	Tonawanda, NY
M5E 1M2	LA1 4XS	U.S.A. 14150

For David and with David, always

CONTENTS

ACKNOWLEDGEMENTS

One of David's greatest gifts as a civic leader and entrepreneur was his ability to attract, inspire, and mobilize legions of talented, committed people, all of whom played important roles in his life and work. Thank you to everyone who inspired David and made it possible for him, in turn, to inspire you. If you were a part of David's life, you are also a part of his story.

I particularly want to acknowledge and thank the many people who helped make this book possible. Some of you are identified by name and some perhaps not enough or not at all. Any resemblance to real persons, living or dead, is generally intentional and any omissions are certainly not.

My first debt of thanks is to Anna Porter, who guided me through the unfamiliar and sometimes terrifying process of writing a memoir and getting it published. You did this initially because David asked you to, but ultimately because you wanted to, and I am grateful for your kindness as well as your friendship.

Thank you to Sylvia Fraser, who worked with me on this memoir by helping me find the words and the way to tell David's story. Anna was right to recommend you as my collaborator, and it was lucky for me that I took her advice. This book would never have happened without you.

Thank you to David Wolfe, whose many conversations with David and transcribed audiotapes provided rich source material for understanding what makes a civic entrepreneur.

Thank you to the many friends and colleagues at The Boston Consulting Group, the Toronto City Summit Alliance (now CivicAction), Luminato, the Governments of Ontario, Canada, and the City of Toronto, along with many other organizations for providing the speeches, videos, articles, and other materials that formed the bedrock for this book.

Thank you to the Burstyn and Pecaut families for sharing your stories and allowing me to share them.

Thank you to the many other friends, family, and colleagues who read this memoir at various stages and offered thoughtful comments, along with honest advice.

And finally, thank you to David for trusting me with this incredibly difficult but ultimately rewarding assignment, and giving us one last chance to work together.

My husband, David Pecaut, has been called a visionary and a pragmatist, fearless and funny, passionate, compassionate, indefatigable, a bridge builder, a catalyst, a dynamo, a trailblazer, and "the smartest person I've ever met" by a variety of other smart people.

Though David was a business leader and management consultant, most of these accolades flowed from his volunteer work. He called himself a civic entrepreneur — someone who convened diverse people of goodwill for the betterment of the community. While David was a native of Sioux City, Iowa, he chose Toronto as the beneficiary of his formidable enthusiasm. He was thrilled by the openness and vibrancy that he discovered on his arrival here in the 1980s, and he wanted to help make Toronto the most socially and culturally dynamic urban centre in the world as a model for other cities.

"No matter what computer is invented, or how powerful, David Pecaut proved the superiority of the human brain in his ability to imagine," said John Tory, David's successor as chair of the Toronto City Summit Alliance, the umbrella group for much of David's pro bono work. "I've heard David described as a popcorn machine of ideas. He also had the rare ability to follow through and to persuade others to rally around. The day I went to his office to recruit him for City Summit was the luckiest day for Toronto in recent civic history."

When Toronto was in the doldrums because of the SARS scare, David helped the city shake its stigma and restore its tourism industry by chairing the Toronto3 Alliance, launched by a flamboyant Rolling Stones rock concert attracting four hundred thousand people. David also co-founded Luminato, the international festival that each spring showcases the world's finest artists to audiences of over a million. "It's a lovely thing when you confide your dreams to someone and that person can imagine them as well as you can," says Karen Kain, artistic director of the National Ballet and a member of Luminato's artistic advisory committee.

David negotiated effectively with every level of government and every political party, both in and out of power. He also worked as easily with the homeless, new immigrants, and poverty activists as with billionaires, cultural czars, corporate CEOs, educators, bank presidents, and labour leaders. Keenly aware of inequality of opportunity, he helped bring educational and social resources to the GTA's poverty pockets with the Strong Neighbourhoods Task Force. He also embraced the Pathways to Education program, flinging university doors open to youth in danger of dropping out or falling prey to gang culture. "He would listen to a lot of chatter — blah blah blah — then pick out the one key point and drive it home," remembers Sam Duboc, chair of Pathways.

David co-chaired Modernizing Income Security for Working Age Adults Task Force with Susan Pigott, CEO of St. Christopher House, an effort that dramatically improved the health and social assistance the federal and Ontario governments would provide for the working poor. "With David, it was always fast-forward," says Susan. "He made a phenomenal difference in improving public policy in a way that directly affected lives. He was also the most generous-spirited person I've ever met."

As a great believer in mentorship, David founded Career Edge, a national youth internship program that has helped ten thousand university and college grads launch their careers. Because he considered immigrants an undervalued resource, he and Ratna Omidvar, president of the Maytree Foundation, a private organization that worked to support immigrants, fight poverty, and build community, founded the Toronto

Region Immigrant Employment Council. TRIEC has helped thousands of skilled newcomers overcome cultural barriers and find work worthy of their talents. This was followed by DiverseCity, an initiative to help visible minorities achieve civic leadership.

David used his knowledge of international markets to help the Toronto Region Research Alliance attract high-tech global companies to the Golden Horseshoe. He also worked with the provincial government to help Ontario position itself as the location of choice for investment. "Every all-star team has a superstar, and that was David," said corporate executive and TRRA chair Courtney Pratt. "Gretzky knew where a puck would go, but David managed to get the puck to go where he wanted it."

Even after David had undergone surgery for colorectal cancer in 2004, he co-chaired Greening Greater Toronto, created to tackle air and water pollution, energy use, and waste disposal. David was determined to make the GTA the greenest area in North America.

In all his enterprises, David credited the people he convened around the table for finding community solutions to community problems. He was always backed by a crack fact-finding team from The Boston Consulting Group (BCG), where he was a senior partner. One BCG colleague described the meeting in which he recruited their support: "He spoke for an hour, no notes, no slides, laying out all the ways we could transform the city, supported by facts that he insisted be of the highest quality. He would never accept hearsay."

David considered anyone useful to a project to be only a phone call away. Alan Broadbent, chair of Maytree, once remarked, "I could imagine David cold-calling the Pope and expecting a call back by the end of the week."

Naki Osutei, project director of the Toronto City Summit Alliance, summed up her experience of David: "I was *Pecauted*, which means someone David has taken from the impossible to the possible in three to five steps, including an action plan."

Many people used "social entrepreneur" to describe David's unique brand of social activism. His ability to connect all the dots, merging personal, professional, and public pursuits, was the hallmark of his civic leadership. David saw himself and others in this mode as "someone who sees the most important thing we do, outside of our families, as the work we do together in building a better society, and doing it collectively."

Globe and Mail feature writer Sandra Martin would later capture David's remarkable range and constant swirl of activity in his obituary: "It is tempting to imagine David Pecaut washing up on a desert island in the South Pacific. He would dry himself off, figure out a way to convene an international summit on global warming, followed by an e-commerce task force on innovative ways to export coconuts. And once he had tapped into the brain waves of his far-flung global partners, he would convince them to join a diversity round table and a mentorship initiative across the diverse economic and social sectors of the minute island," she wrote. "Naturally, he would persuade a series of strong, capable women to run these projects. Then he would blue sky an annual cultural festival that would attract tourism dollars, enhance local artistic standards, and build international audiences. And he would do all of this for free, earning nothing more than the praise of the islanders and the satisfaction of making his island a more innovative, competitive and diverse place." David would have enjoyed that description of himself.

———————

Because I worked professionally and lived daily with David, I knew both his public and private selves. Contrary to widespread rumour that he had no "off switch," he did know how to relax, but usually in an energetic way — playing basketball in our driveway, jogging a few kilometres, or riffing on the piano, perhaps with a baby on his lap. We had four daughters, two that came as a bonus with me when we married and two that followed. He was a remarkable father — always accessible, always playful, always bursting with knowledge that he was happy to share. His many quirks were a continuing source of affectionate family teasing: his perpetual singing, his obliviousness to decorating changes, his storehouse of arcane information, his total lack of interest in material things, his inability to match one shoe with the other. Fashion was his victim.

David was the perfect life partner. He retained his childlike sense of wonder about everything and everybody. It was impossible for David to talk to anyone without coming up with a fascinating piece of information or an idea that might be woven into some grand scheme. He was a lightning strike, a force of nature, but his priorities were always real and constant. No matter how high he might fly, it was always his family first, then friends and community. We kept him from flying too close to the sun.

In the natural order of events, David would have written his own memoir. When it became obvious even to him, the supreme optimist, that his time was running out, he began to make copious notes in the spidery hand only a few of us could decipher. He eagerly recorded interviews with friends, colleagues, and family, including me and our daughters. When his lungs became so choked by cancer that he could barely speak, he whispered and coughed out his words because he still had so many things he wanted to say.

Throughout his life, David was always in a hurry, always planning and doing at a frenetic pace. The very end of his life could not have been more different. He was serene and composed, loath to leave us but ready to enter the next life. David died peacefully at home on December 14, 2009, surrounded by his adoring family and mourned by his many friends.

CHAPTER ONE

The Mythical Man

I met David Pecaut because the political winds in Ontario changed course. In June 1985, Ontario had elected its first Liberal government in forty-two years. On the crest of this surprise victory, Premier David Peterson had decided that the province needed a new industrial policy to position it as a competitive force in an increasingly global economy.

I was a senior policy advisor for the Ontario government's Premier's Council Secretariat, and David was a partner at Telesis, the Rhode Island consulting firm that had been hired, together with the Canada Consulting Group (CCG), to conduct a landmark study of the Ontario economy.

From December 1986, when I joined the council, I had heard about this mythical team leader, David Pecaut. The reason I thought him a myth was because he never attended a meeting. Either he was in Rhode Island, where he lived, or travelling the world for other clients. Every time we gathered around a table, members of the CCG team would ask over and over, "What would David do?" or simply "Where the hell is David?" The rest of us would just wonder if David existed.

It wasn't until February 1987, three months later, that David Pecaut actually did come to a meeting. He was late. Eight of us waited in anticipation, punctuating every discussion with the phrase "When David gets here …"

We waited an hour. His flight — who knows from where! — had been delayed. When our high-powered consultant finally did arrive, he was sweating, his tie was thrown over his shoulder, he desperately needed a haircut, and he was carrying about six Loblaws shopping bags — one bag for each of his current multi-million-dollar clients, as I would later learn. He plunked everything down. Then, instead of some version of "I'm sorry I'm late," he began with an impatient challenge: "So what have you been doing?"

It was not a good meeting. Most of us on the government team were experiencing him for the first time, and now we were expected to run off and do something else for the project without really knowing what that was. I left feeling mildly disgruntled and thinking, *I don't like this guy.*

The Premier's Council — an independent body of high-ranking business and community leaders, along with key economic cabinet ministers — had been proposed by Patrick Lavelle, Ontario's deputy minister of industry, along with Neil Paget, a Canada Consulting Group partner, and David. The first condition for success was that Premier Peterson demonstrate his seriousness by earmarking a significant sum to implement the council's findings. The premier established a $1-billion technology fund, then confirmed the second condition for success: that he personally invest his time by chairing every meeting and making Ontario's industrial policy a top priority.

Peterson had no trouble enlisting a heterogeneous group of heavy hitters from the business, academic, and labour communities. These were not just representatives, but leaders who could make bold decisions and deliver results. The million-dollar contract to do the research and develop the report was won jointly by the Canada Consulting Group and Telesis.

As a member of the research team on the government side, I was initially responsible for analyzing two sectors: aerospace and biotech. My second meeting with David Pecaut was a one-on-one where he was to review my work. Typically, he arrived late, coffee cup in hand, tie loosened, shirt rumpled, sleeves rolled up, and still in need of a haircut.

In the consulting world, information is presented in slides, each consisting of a headline declaring the main idea, backed up by a few bullet points, a graph, or a chart.

David began flipping through my aerospace deck, looking perplexed and slightly disdainful. He paused at one slide, barely looking up. "Why is this here?"

"Well, I'm trying to compare the size of our industry to what there is in the U.S."

"You couldn't find any current data? This stuff is at least ten years old. It's useless."

After a few more terse exchanges, he shut the deck and looked me squarely in the eye. "What did you study in college?"

"English Literature." I did not feel it wise to boast that my Coles Notes on *Macbeth*, designed to help students cram for exams, had been a bestseller.

"*Where* did you go to college?"

"Windsor for undergrad, McMaster and U of T for post-grad."

He was clearly unimpressed. "So, what are you doing in industry, trade and technology?"

"I saw an ad for a senior policy advisor for this new thing called the Premier's Council, I was interested, and I applied."

He rolled his eyes. "Oh, great, they've given me an English major!"

Ironically, David's own formal education was also in the liberal arts. He had never taken a business or an economics course in his life. Of course, I didn't know that at the time. What I did know was that this guy was behaving like a jerk, and for me the meeting was over.

I began repacking my briefcase while he watched with a slightly alarmed look. "What are you doing?"

I replied with dead calm, "This is what I've done. I have more work to do. I'll see you at the next meeting. Maybe."

Much later, he told me that he vaguely remembered that our session had not been very successful, but that he had been personally intrigued by me.

Working with David wasn't part of my job description, and I didn't want to deal with someone who was so clearly dismissive of me, and was rude enough to say so. I had an excellent professional relationship with Neil Paget, David's senior partner at CCG, so I chose to work with him.

Meanwhile, I was attending council and team meetings where David was the star performer. It didn't take long for everyone around the table to appreciate his genius as a presenter and storyteller. He was so comfortable with complexity, so skilled at proposing and explaining big ideas, and so adept at distilling vast deposits of data into useful knowledge.

David believed that his biggest contributions to the Premier's Council, aside from helping develop the policies it implemented, was introducing a common language that bridged a real gap between the private sector and the trade unions. For David, the right shared language would make or break the project: "If you talked about it as an issue of productivity, the labour leadership immediately assumed that this is about work speed-ups, faster production lines, all of the things we've fought all our lives. But if you said that we can increase wages only by getting higher value added productivity per employee, by working smarter, employing capital more effectively, and getting higher prices for our products, they could buy into that." This allowed council members like Leo Gerard, Ontario head of the United Steelworkers of America, to agree with Paul Phoenix, president of Dofasco Inc., that labour was a vital partner in boosting productivity.

The premier had set the ground rules by telling everyone at the table, "You're not here wearing a particular hat of this manufacturer's association or that union. You're here as an individual to grapple with facts and to learn what's really going on and to deal with these issues through consensus." An early consensus was our recognition that Canada, and especially Ontario, could no longer rely on low-cost raw materials or on being wage-competitive with countries like China. Instead, our future prosperity relied on developing a knowledge-based, innovative economy. Though this is common wisdom today, it was cutting-edge thinking in the 1980s.

Also revolutionary was David's belief that it was more important to invest in traded companies that competed globally than companies that served only local markets. Even though non-traded companies might employ more people in a community, it was the success of traded companies that mattered most to the economy. He used the example of an Ontario town that has a steel mill along with factories that provide consumer goods. If one of the local factories closes, the others would likely pick up the business, recirculating the wealth. But if the mill fails, everyone in town would be seriously affected because the mill brings in outside money, and its jobs cannot be replaced by other local activity.

David also understood that traded companies establish the value of services in other, non-traded sectors. A barber in Mexico may be a better stylist than one in New York, but it's the wealth created by traded goods and services that determines the value of his work and the income he will earn.

David believed that stories were as powerful as data in making the case for a policy shift, program support, or an agenda change, and he was adept at summoning the right anecdotal evidence from his own experience.

David regaled the Premier's Council and other clients with stories of his work with the Israeli government to illustrate the value of building on export strengths rather than shoring up local businesses. Telesis had persuaded the Israeli government to focus on companies already gaining global attention, instead of placing plants in disadvantaged regions. Telesis had also engaged Israel's powerful Diaspora in developing export markets through branding, distribution, and investment. This had resulted in Marks & Spencer becoming a major importer of Israeli fashions and in the establishment of Israel's venture capital industry.

One of the strategy's most successful features was making the Office of the Chief Scientist a focal point for research and development, and encouraging Israel to develop bi-national agreements that funded Israeli companies to work with partners like Motorola or Intel in Europe and the United States. The process worked because it was non-partisan and engaged leadership from both Labour and Likud. It helped that this was 1986, a relatively peaceful time. But the stormy political realities of internal Israeli politics occasionally intruded.

David told the story of how the Telesis team was taken to a bunker in Jerusalem where they would be meeting Prime Minister Shimon Peres and his cabinet for the first time. David was surprised that the young men flanking him didn't speak English — until one leaned forward and he spied an UZI under his jacket. Despite the friendliness of the steering committee and all the frisking for this meeting, David was still considered a security risk.

Another very political moment occurred during a TV show established to debate the export strategy report. Peres began with a very articulate, very positive description of its contents, simultaneously translated for David. This was followed by a statement from Ariel Sharon, his political opponent, also stating his strong support. After that, David's translator fell silent while Peres and Sharon fired back and forth.

David kept asking, "What are they saying?"

His translator shrugged. "They've forgotten the report. They're just attacking each other."

———————

While the work of the council progressed, David's and my personal relationship followed its own rambling course.

One evening our consulting team took a break from all our hard work to go to a baseball game. Somehow, I ended up giving David a lift down to Exhibition Stadium. He was curious, on opening my car trunk to stow his coat and suitcase, about the paper bags of canned goods and other non-perishables. When I explained that I was intending to drop them off at a fire hall for the food bank, he said, "That's something my mother would do." I didn't know then that his mother was one of his icons, but he looked at me with fresh interest and perhaps a bit of embarrassment.

On our first "date" in the spring of 1988, David took me to lunch at the College Park food court.

That began with the sound of a throat being cleared at my office door. Since my back was turned, I had to look around to see who was there.

"Have you had lunch?" asked David.

"Not yet," I responded tersely, and returned to my computer. You see, I still didn't like him much.

"Do you want to grab a bite?" he persisted.

I paused before turning to face him again. "If you can wait ten minutes."

I took the full ten minutes, maybe more, while he waited patiently outside my office door. Then we walked the short distance to the food court. En route, he asked, "Are you going anywhere for Easter?"

"I'm driving down the coast of California with a friend. He's planning the whole trip, and has booked tickets for us to see Hearst Castle."

David howled with laughter. "Don't you just drive up the hill and buy your tickets?"

"My friend likes to book just to make sure."

David wouldn't leave it alone. "How spontaneous! What does your friend do?"

"He's a journalist."

During lunch at the food court, David asked all sorts of questions about me and my family. He seemed fascinated that my parents were Holocaust survivors, and that my father and his two friends had married three sisters so they could always stay together. He also told me about growing up in Sioux City, Iowa, and especially about Great-Great-Grandfather Gustav from Switzerland, one of the American Midwest's first white settlers.

He told me that he was living in Rhode Island with a woman from Toronto, whom he had met while studying philosophy at the University of Sussex. She was Jewish. He said he always seemed to date Jewish woman.

I told him that I was a single mother with two small daughters, which didn't seem to perturb him. Then he asked me three questions that demonstrated how very American — or, at least, un-Canadian — he was.

"So how do you vote?"

I hedged: "Uh, Liberal. I'm from an immigrant family. It's hereditary."

"What did your father do for a living?"

He was clearly fishing for my economic status. "He was a small business owner." David liked that. His father was also self-employed, as a stockbroker.

It was the third question that really got me: "So how much does a government job like yours pay?"

Outrageous! "Well enough."

I had ordered an egg salad sandwich, David a tuna one. Half of mine was left on the plate, untouched.

David eyed it longingly. "Aren't you going to eat that?"

"No, help yourself."

I hadn't finished my drink either.

"Aren't you going to finish that juice?"

"No, go ahead."

He had a voracious appetite, so he ate and talked, and talked and ate. His stories were fascinating; I could have listened a lot longer. He also paid careful attention to what I had to say. After two hours of non-stop conversation I decided that David Pecaut was actually quite a sweet character — despite his rudeness and the stains on his tie and the food on his chin.

In the weeks that followed, David and I privately acknowledged that we might be interested in becoming a couple. The pace of our romantic involvement was affected by the fact that we were rarely in the same city, even the same hemisphere. David was commuting to Australia once a month, working on a national strategy for the Australian Manufacturing Association. When he wasn't in Australia, he was in Europe or Asia or somewhere far enough away that his calls would usually come in the middle of the night. I never minded waking up to speak to him.

We had some spirited arguments during this period over seemingly trivial subjects. One was about the film *Amadeus*. I liked it, David didn't. He thought the character of Mozart excessive and cartoonish, which was fair enough, except that he challenged me in a way that suggested I lacked the formidable intellect necessary to appreciate good art. We both stood our ground, emerging with a fair measure of respect for ourselves and each other.

David later defined this as a "proxy argument," during which we were defining who we would be as a couple.

A key task of the Premier's Council was to analyze provincial industries and assess their global competitiveness, along with the government's economic policies, such as tax barriers and business location incentives.

In an effort to grow more Canadian-based multinationals, the council focused on threshold companies, defined as those with sales in the range of $40 million to $400 million, with a significant percentage in exports. Often these flew under the radar, were underfunded, and were endangered by their own creativity, since the cost of launching a new product might mean betting the company. The council identified some twenty-five promising companies that were poised to be become strong global players. One was auto parts manufacturer Magna International. While Magna's sales were over the preferred limit, the company was competing against much larger multinationals. Years later, Magna fulfilled its promise by becoming a major multinational and a huge Canadian success story.

When developing the concept for what would become the Centres of Excellence, the council asked, "What companies with deep capability already exist here in Ontario?" To be a Centre of Excellence, sector partners had to demonstrate not only that they were on the cutting edge in new technologies but also that they were prepared to co-invest. Based on the council's recommendation, the Peterson government created an open competition, led by a high-powered international panel, to evaluate proposals. One winner was the Water Technology Centre in the Guelph-Kitchener region. Before the competition, few people knew that Ontario was an innovator in groundwater research. A plan was developed for the Centre, with the result that Ontario became recognized as a world leader in water research.

The Premier's Council was not immune to outside forces. When the fractious free trade debate threatened to split the group, Premier Peterson declared, "Free trade is off the table. I know some of you have strong views, and I'll talk to you about those in private, but what we're achieving here is too important to be undermined or sidelined."

Everybody accepted that decision. The council proved it could maintain a focus and achieve consensus despite clashing attitudes on broader issues.

To create the Premier's Council report, those of us on the government team were responsible for submitting chapters about our sectors, on the assumption that these, like other CCG reports, would be contracted out to a professional writer. After reading my slide deck, which I'd transformed into prose, Neil Paget declared, "We have a writer!"

Apparently, my English degree — previously an object of ridicule — might be of value after all.

I found myself working even more closely with David during the report-writing phase. The two of us would hover around the printer, waiting for the latest pages to pop out and competing to see who could grab them first. Then we would stay up all hours fighting about what the report should say. It wasn't just about who had the last word; it was about getting the best ideas on paper and expressing them well. I knew how to capture David's voice and how to commit to paper the best stories and examples that he summoned so effortlessly in his presentations and speeches. Neil Paget later joked that the report turned out so right because I was the only one who could outlast David, but in fact we wrote it together. Nothing like this report had ever been done before — not in Ontario and not in Canada — and our intense collaboration was one of the keys to its success.

The study, entitled *Competing in the New Global Economy*, was completed in 1988. It was 250 pages, with 14 recommendations. These included an Ontario Recapitalization Incentive Plan to support indigenous, mid-sized exporting companies; an Ontario Risk Sharing Fund for matching loans for product development for export; tax incentives to encourage investment in promising ventures; and tax incentives for research and development. Our second report, *People and Skills in the New Global Economy*, would later recommend mechanisms for engaging key stakeholders in traded companies in restructuring plans; retraining for workers undergoing technological change; and investments in education, skills training, and lifelong learning.

That first report was the culmination of a huge team effort, for which David credited the power of those around the table. He was especially pleased with Peterson's commitment. As he stated, "The Premier seemed to love the meetings and the way we put the fact base together, analyzing all the sectors of the economy with vigour. It was a terrific process!"

There was one meeting with the premier, Pat Lavelle, David, and Neil that stands out, but for personal reasons. At that time, only a few people — including Neil, but not the premier — knew David and I were involved.

David was briefing Peterson with his usual passion and rapid-fire pace. Suddenly, the premier interrupted, "Pecaut!"

David stopped.

"You need a haircut."

"Yeah, I know, I usually wait till I come to Toronto because I like my barber, Danny, but I haven't had chance to see him in a while."

David resumed his briefing.

"Pecaut!"

David stopped again.

"You have a hole in your shoe."

David looked down. "Oh, yeah, I really need to get that fixed."

Peterson turned to me in mock exasperation, "Can't you do something with this guy, maybe take care of him — or are you still seeing that other guy?"

David and I froze, but Neil didn't miss a beat, "Well, actually, Premier, it's a bought deal."

Peterson either didn't hear or didn't understand Neil's comment, because when David and I *did* go public, he was mildly annoyed that we hadn't told him earlier. However, he later began taking credit for having suggested our liaison in the first place, with this endorsement: "One of the best things to come out of the Premier's Council!"

This anecdote has a postscript.

When it came time to launch *Competing in the New Global Economy*, the premier strongly believed that it should be presented by various prominent people on his council, and just the highlights, without too much content.

I argued that there was a place for content too. "Pecaut is by far our best presenter. Why don't you do the intro, then have a few of the council's leading lights speak about the key findings, then have David present some slides with deeper content?"

The premier shot back, "Nobody wants a lot of facts shoved at them. It's a press conference."

I persisted. "This is different. People will sit longer and pay more attention because this is really interesting and important. You can fire me if it doesn't work out."

Suddenly, Peterson stopped arguing. "Wait a second. Are you sleeping with Pecaut?"

"No," I replied indignantly, then added under my breath, "Not yet."

Finally, he conceded, "Fine, do it your way, but it better be good."

It wasn't good, it was great. David delivered a virtuoso performance, complete with an encyclopedic display of facts and an amazing array of stories about what strategies had worked for Australia's auto industry and Israel's export markets. The audience, including the media, sat enraptured for over an hour.

Competing in the New Global Economy immediately became government policy. When Premier Peterson sent a copy of the report to Nobel laureate and economist Robert Solow, he received back a personal letter in which Solow stated that it was the best articulation of economic challenges and solutions that he had ever read.

The Premier's Council's model for Centres of Excellence was later replicated in Europe and Australia, and the council itself became the subject of a number of academic theses on how to set economic policy.

As for David, he always maintained that his greatest satisfaction had been the opportunity to create common ground for government, industry, and labour, as well as to change the way government thought and talked about the economy.

CHAPTER TWO

Mergers, Personal and Professional

A fter the launch of the 1988 Premier's Council report, David decided to move from Rhode Island to Toronto. As he enthused to a Canadian immigration officer at Pearson International Airport, "I want to make Canada my permanent home."

The officer stared at him in surprise, "You've got an American passport and you want to move *here*? If I had that, I'd be out of this country in a flash."

David exclaimed, "I can't believe you said that! I want to live in Toronto. It's a fantastic city and one day it will be the best in the world."

David had fallen in love with Toronto seven years earlier when he arrived here from Sioux City, age twenty-seven, with all of his belongings stashed in a rusty Dodge Colt. He had expected something like Cleveland, or maybe Hamilton, with its jagged line of smokestacks, but approaching the city from the Queen Elizabeth Way filled him with excitement. He missed Toronto during the three years he subsequently spent commuting from his job at Telesis in Providence. He thought this city had unlimited potential, and now he wanted to settle here.

David was still partnered with the Toronto woman whom he'd met while attending Sussex University, then lived with in Rhode Island. He said that the relationship had been troubled for a long time but — to use his own expression — he felt stuck. I'm the sort of person who makes up my mind quickly. I had never before encountered anyone like David, and I had no trouble deciding this was the guy with whom I wanted to spend my life. It wasn't just his enthusiasm, his warmth, or the fact that he was one of the smartest people I'd ever known — it was the whole package. He talked so freely about his family and everything else that I felt I'd come to know him well in a short time.

Eventually, David became unstuck, and he moved into a third-floor flat on Roxborough East. I had introduced my daughters, Lauren and Amy, to him when they were eight and five. He wasn't at all fazed that he had fallen in love with a woman with two children and an intimidating ex-husband who was still part of their lives. David was wonderful with the girls, always playful and fun. Amy fell in love with him immediately — a relationship he sealed by bringing her a different stuffed animal each time he returned from Australia, with the species becoming ever more exotic. Lauren, who was more reticent, took a bit longer to warm up. David also went out of his way to be friendly with Ron, my ex-husband, and whenever Ron came to pick up the girls he talked more to David than to me. Though they were never going to be pals, they were very comfortable with each other.

By the time we were working on a second Premier's Council report, keeping our relationship secret had become a strain, especially since we had many close friends on, or connected to, the council. I had told a few people, and a few others had grown suspicious when David and I took our vacation at the same time in order to go backpacking in Kluane National Park, a mountainous backbone between the Yukon and Alaska. David had been surprised when I agreed, because he didn't think Jewish girls liked hiking and camping, and he thought I was faking enthusiasm to impress him.

Our hikes were long, rugged, and difficult. David was frankly surprised at my stamina and genuine love of the outdoors. It was a wonderful adventure, during which we explored unspoiled wilderness trails through lush valleys and sweeping ice fields, wearing cowbells on our knapsacks to scare away the black bears we might encounter.

When we returned, we faced the difficult prospect of going public about our relationship. David proved uncharacteristically timid, leaving it to me to break the news to Deputy Minister Patrick Lavelle, his client and my boss. That happened over lunch at Winston's. When I told Pat that his two protégés were now a couple, he almost choked on his smoked salmon, quickly downed a glass of water, and eyed the nearest exit.

Pat was not disapproving, as we later learned, just taken off guard. He recovered quickly, and he and his wife, Linda, became very close friends. We had much the same reaction from our colleagues, once they got over their surprise.

One day in August 1989, David and I were walking along Roxborough Street East, where he was living. We happened upon an open house and, on impulse, we went inside. By the time we left, we'd decided to put in an offer on the property.

I sold my place in Bayview Village more quickly than either of us expected. David — who had never owned a house, who had never invested in anything other than the stock market, and who still thought our relationship was exploratory — was hesitant. "Is this what we really want to do?"

I told him, "If things don't work out, then they don't. But they will."

And they did, though for a long time afterwards, David would scratch his head and tease, "When was it again that we decided to get married?" He always marvelled that I was quick to decide and act on everything, whereas he took longer. He hated the idea of making a decision he would come to regret. He told me later, and often, that marrying me was the only decision in his life that had never given him a moment's regret.

David moved into our new home that September, and the girls and I joined him during their March break. We instantly became a family, though the wedding would not take place until several months later.

David took me to Sioux City to meet his parents in the fall of 1989. I waited anxiously at Pearson International Airport while our flight was called over and over, then listened fearfully to the announcement that the gates were closing. That's when David arrived, sweating and dishevelled.

He'd cut his time too close while making a presentation, and now he was upset with the flight attendants for barring us from boarding.

Sioux City was difficult to fly to at any time, but since David had a habit of missing planes, he was adept at jockeying schedules and coming up with alternatives. We ended up in Omaha, Nebraska, at eleven at night with a ninety-minute drive to Sioux City ahead of us. While we waited for our rental car, we had an affectionate moment in the airport — nothing more than a kiss. A state trooper happened to be walking by and chastised us, "This is a family place. We don't allow that kind of behaviour here." I thought he was kidding, but David tapped my arm in warning. The trooper was, indeed, serious. I began to wonder if all of the Midwest, including the Pecaut home, was a no-kissing zone. I was also concerned that I might bear some of the blame for our lateness.

It was after midnight when we arrived in Sioux City. David's mother, Dorothy, met us at the door in her dressing gown. She was expecting David to stay in his old room, and had prepared a separate one for me. David told her, "No, we want to stay together," and she accepted that after a brief hesitation.

Dottie was a lovely woman with delicate features, an athletic build, prematurely grey hair, bright blue eyes, and a radiant smile. She turned out to be one of the kindest, most genuine people I've ever met. And she was fun. I loved her sparkle. She never tried to impress anyone, but she always did. David's stockbroker father, Dick, was a trim man with neatly parted greying hair and a hearty laugh. Both parents were active tennis players and golfers, and both were pillars of church and community.

In typical honesty, David had informed them that my divorce wasn't final. Though by then I'd been separated and supporting myself for four years, my child support arrangements had not yet been determined. I was also insistent on applying for a Jewish divorce, which turned out to be easier than the court one. Though Dick and Dottie were troubled at first about my marital situation, after asking a few probing questions and receiving what must have been reassuring answers from me, they were gracious and welcoming.

I shouldn't have worried about being blamed for our missing our flight. David's family knew all too well that he was late for everything — school projects, dental appointments, buses, trains, and, yes, planes. Since our relationship was still defining itself, I let him get away with it. Later, we reached an accommodation. If David was travelling for business, he could miss as many flights as he wanted, but for family vacations, he had to play by family rules. After missing a couple of those as well, he realized the grief I made him endure was just not worth it.

For Christmas of that same year, we took a second trip to Sioux City, this time with the children. By then, my divorce was final, and the Pecauts had planned a big engagement party for us with friends and neighbours. Since my luggage hadn't arrived, I borrowed shoes and a skirt from Dottie. She was impressed by how unperturbed I was, and she later told me she believed my composure brought a much-needed sense of calm to an often-agitated David.

The kids' excitement over the trip proved well-founded. Dottie had a superb sense of occasion, and her Christmas festivities, featuring cookies to be decorated with coloured icing, taught our family how to celebrate. Relatives and friends congregated in the living room of the Pecauts' big red brick house with its pillared porch, with the same warmth and easy camaraderie as the Cleavers in *Leave It to Beaver*.

David and I were married on June 2, 1990. David, who was over-the-top generous, took me to Paris to buy the perfect dress. After two days of searching, we found it on Rue du Faubourg Saint-Honoré in the window of a tiny designer shop with only five or six dresses, each unique. The instant I put it on, we both knew it was the one. It was a black sheath with a multicoloured silk over-blouse that fell just below my knees. David wore a handsome black suit with a subtle periwinkle stripe, a white shirt, and a matching periwinkle tie — all picked by me, and not anything he could describe or fully appreciate, since he had a limited ability to distinguish colours.

The morning of the wedding, six-year-old Amy came pounding down the stairs from the third floor and jumped on David, pummelling his chest and screaming, "You're not my father! You'll never be my father! You're a … a … turtle!"

David replied with touching diplomacy, "Then I'll be your turtle."

That was all the reassurance she needed to calm her anxiety.

Our nondenominational ceremony took place at city hall. Jay Ingram, David's first friend in Toronto, was the best man, and my longtime friend Linda Rechtsman was my matron of honour. Neither David nor I was religious, but we asked Judge Sydney Harris, father of a friend, to officiate, since having a Jewish judge would show respect for my heritage and please my family. Afterwards, we celebrated in our beautiful garden with seventy-five close friends and relatives.

———

The second report of the Premier's Council was published in 1990. Called *People and Skills in the New Global Economy*, it stressed the need to create opportunity through a culture of continuous education. As well as providing the province with an educational blueprint from elementary school to university, it called for the establishment of local training centres to prepare workers to compete in the evolving marketplace.

On September 6, David Peterson's Liberal government fell to Bob Rae's NDP party, and the fate of the Premier's Council became uncertain. By then, the Canada Consulting Group of Toronto had been purchased by Towers Perrin, another consulting firm. David, who had once worked for CCG, had an ambitious plan to broker a merger between that company and The Boston Consulting Group, a world leader in business and strategy consulting.

The situation was a complicated one. Not only would David have to purchase a majority share in CCG from Towers Perrin, but he would also have to persuade the current CCG partners to buy in with him. That meant positioning the deal as a genuine merger, not a takeover where CCG would be swamped and their brand would disappear.

David also had to persuade powerful BCG that this Canadian company was worth their efforts. BCG's thinking was: Why should we merge with CCG instead of just hiring Pecaut, as we've already offered to do? David needed to convince them that CCG, as well as punching well above its weight, was a Canadian "heritage property" that should be preserved. He was aided by George Stalk of BCG, who was also committed to co-founding the new company as BCG's first Canadian office.

By January 1, 1992, the two companies had agreed in principle to a merger. As David noted, "We all came out of the protracted negotiation with an incredible feeling that the world was our oyster."

After David's and my personal merger, our most important collaboration produced two more daughters. During our courtship, it was an early signal for both of us when David asked if I would be interested in having more children, and I replied, "Absolutely!" His eyes lit up, and the pace of our courtship quickened. I became pregnant in the first year of our marriage. Sarah was born in August 1991, Becca in September 1993.

David could not have been more excited about and involved in my pregnancies. Sometimes it seemed as if we were both "big with child." If he could have taken turns carrying the baby, I'm convinced he would have.

After David and I were married, his CCG partner Neil Paget wryly observed that, despite David's global travels, he would always be home when it mattered because his new family created a strong "competing market." Neil was right. David attended all my prenatal classes, studied up on the birth process, and became so expert that he actually wanted to do the delivery.

Because of my previous two pregnancies, I already had a highly competent obstetrician, whom David now wanted to meet. I warned him that she was not warm, nor even necessarily likable. Though she loved delivering babies, she seemed somewhat oblivious to their mothers and was very good at ignoring their fathers altogether. Oh, and she was a relentless chain-smoker. As we sat in her office, in clouds of cigarette fumes, David asked her if I should take any special health precautions, such as cutting down on my coffee intake. Her answer sent him into shock: "Helen should probably limit herself to four cups a day."

Though everything worked out well with Sarah's delivery, we were happy that this obstetrician was out of town at a conference during Becca's birth. And David actually did get to deliver her!

After the attending doctor did a quick examination, she concluded that I was hours away from giving birth and went for dinner, leaving David and me alone with our very lovely and highly engaged labour room nurse. I immediately asked for an epidural, knowing from pregnancies past that this would bring on labour in no time. It did. David came up with a charming description of Becca's speedy birth: "She shot out like a rocket, and I caught her like a football."

That was pretty accurate, and his mixed metaphor made it a memorable piece of family lore. We never did get from the labour room into the delivery room, and I didn't have to do much of anything — just one push, and David and Becca did the rest, ably assisted by our labour nurse. When the doctor returned from dinner, she was clearly annoyed that we had gone ahead without her, but the rest of us were elated. David cradled this baby that he had longed to deliver, with her large, perfectly shaped head, and he was thrilled. He always took such delight in our babies, whether he was changing diapers, bathing them, bouncing them on his belly, or singing silly songs to them.

Our older daughters were also excited. With both Sarah and Becca, it was love at first sight. We joked that, as babies, their feet barely touched the floor because they were held and cuddled constantly, and tossed up in the air frequently. Their delight in being airborne was surely something they inherited from their dad.

Even before Becca's birth, David and I had decided we needed a larger house. Our shopping list consisted of another bedroom, a family room, a main-floor washroom, a garden as beautiful as the one we had, and — this was a desperate desire on David's part — a driveway like the one where he grew up, perfect for shooting hoops. Basketball was always high on David's list of must-haves.

I was dispatched to find a house with these qualifications. After looking at about twenty prospects, I narrowed the list to three before summoning David back from a business trip in Europe for the kill. I knew for certain the one I wanted, but I also knew by then that David liked things better if they were his idea. After telling him that any of the three candidates could be the one, I showed him the other two first. He walked through them with a furrowed brow and a running commentary: *This one seems too dark, that one needs a lot of work, not enough backyard here for the kids to play.*

When we visited the third house, David walked wordlessly through every room, completing his tour in ten minutes. Then, after one more turn around the kitchen, he announced with certainty, "Let's put in an offer."

This rambling, century-old Rosedale house had no for sale sign out front and was not yet officially on the market, but we bought it that day, and moved in ten days before Becca was born.

The move proved an ordeal. August 26, 1993, was one of the hottest days on record, and David was conspicuously out of town for most of it. When he finally showed up at eight in the evening, the movers were still at it, and he immediately became officious: Why, he wanted to know, was a three-block job taking so long? What had these incompetent guys been doing all day? And, by the way, was there any dinner left for him?

Here was the same jerk who had arrived late for his first Premier's Council meeting, then demanded to know what his team had done during his absence. It was lucky for him that I was speechless, and too exhausted to fight back. Since I was eight months pregnant with Becca, I was staying very still so as not to go into labour. In fact, I think the rush of all that day's activity might explain why Becca decided to arrive early.

CHAPTER THREE

Eleven Out of Ten

B ecause David loved his family and loved to talk, it was easy to learn his life story and impossible not to.

He was born in Sioux City, Iowa, on September 14, 1955, two weeks late, and with his arrival induced by castor oil — a procrastinator then, as he always would be. He began to talk at around nine months, then never stopped. His first word — the beginning of a precocious vocabulary — was "tractor," reflecting his community's rural roots. His first ambition, stated at a kid's locally televised birthday party, was to be a garbage man. As proof of this intention, he would get up early on garbage days to run down the street and pull lids off trash cans, curious to see what treasures he could acquire while assisting the garbage collectors.

An incident during a family visit to his maternal grandparents in Chicago proved more indicative of David's ultimate career choice. After he disappeared, at age five, in the Chicago train station, a frantic search found him sitting on the steps of a Pullman car, surrounded by a half-dozen porters. He was interviewing them in the same frank fashion he would later use to question me: *Do you make much money? Oh, that's too bad. Then you must really like trains.* Even then, he loved talking to people and hearing their stories. He was also keenly curious about how things worked. He remembered standing in the train's WC with his brother, Dan, flushing and re-flushing the toilet to see the tracks.

David's childhood was happy in every way.

His parents, Richard Pecaut and Dorothy Kent, met at Iowa State University, where Dick was attending the business school and Dottie was studying home economics journalism. They were married in 1953, then spent two years living in Virginia and in Morocco, where Dick was posted as a naval lieutenant. In 1955, Dick joined his father, Russell, at C.W. Britton, a securities firm that had managed to survive the stock market crash and the Depression. After five years, Dick, his brother Jack, and their father founded the family investment firm of Pecaut & Company. Though it was a bold step, they surprised themselves by making money from the first day.

Sioux City is a charming farm-to-market community on the Missouri River with a current population of 83,000. It's set in rolling hills and valleys that also define the city. Dick and Dottie had their four children with assembly-line efficiency — David in 1955; Daniel, sixteen months later, in 1957; Stacey in 1958, and Mary Michelle (called Shelley by the family) in 1959. They raised them on tree-lined Valley Drive in the same upper-middle-class neighbourhood where Dick had grown up. Their four-bedroom house with its white-pillared porch, French windows, and lovely garden was comfortably and traditionally furnished. A basketball hoop over the garage was a staple of life for their four kids, along with a side yard that served as the neighbourhood football field and never grew grass because of all the trampling feet.

David and his brother were especially close. As Dan recalled, "David was my hero. Wherever he was I wanted to be, and whatever he was doing I wanted to do. Before we started school, I doubt I even knew who I was apart from David. We spent nearly every waking hour together, living inside our imaginations. We were a unit. Mom said I didn't speak much until I was three. David had all that covered."

Since the two boys shared bunk beds, with David in the lower one, Dan's day began with a brotherly thump in the back. Then it was breakfast, play, fight; lunch, play, fight; dinner, bath, more play, this time with bubbles and boats, then bed — the most challenging adventure of all. That was because the bogeyman lived under the bunk, with a two-foot radius of influence, meaning the brothers had to leap to safety. But wait, often a swamp with alligators filled the middle of the room, requiring them to climb onto the dresser, then the bookcase, before diving under the covers. Once in bed, they had their own goodnight ritual. First they'd say their prayers, then they'd tell each other, "I love you," then they'd blow each other a kiss. When each one had replied, "I got it," it was time for sleep.

This ritual continued until grade school, when the brothers learned a sad fact of peer-group life: only girls kissed.

After the Pecaut daughters were old enough to join their brothers in play, the four siblings would build stores, perform shows, and reinvent the rules of board games. The boys usually won, frequently by cheating. David, by his own confession, could be a bit of a bully, pretending to throw his sisters' dolls down the clothes chute and other obnoxious brotherly pranks. As an adult, he felt guilty enough about having harassed his sisters to offer a long overdue apology.

One day, when David was, as usual, chasing ten-year-old Dan around the house, Dan spun back and punched his big brother in the mouth — more shock than hurt for both of them. That was a moment of liberation for Dan, marking a shift in their relationship. Then, in high school, Dan had the good sense to grow taller than his "big" brother so that David could no longer best him, one-on-one, in basketball. Dan confessed that it made him sad to beat his hero, but being a Pecaut he preferred to win.

A lifetime skill that David demonstrated early was the art of manipulation. If he wanted something, he'd invent a game that would seduce his siblings into competing to please him. Once, while all four were watching cartoons, David needed a Kleenex. He challenged, "Let's have a race to see who can bring me a Kleenex the fastest." Of course, the real winner was David, who ended up with three Kleenexes without missing a single frame of the cartoon.

David displayed a genius for inversion, the same way Tom Sawyer turned the nuisance of whitewashing a fence into a valuable opportunity. One winter's day, Dottie was dismayed to see Dan and Stacey shovelling a neighbour's driveway with David supervising. He was paying each a penny, while pocketing the hefty difference. That, according to Dan, was how David discovered the profit margin advantage of being in management.

On another occasion, an exasperated Dottie tried to shame her brood into improving their table manners by fashioning a paper plate, called Mr. Manners, to be worn around the neck of the loser. Instead, David turned Mr. Manners into a trophy to be won. He proceeded to talk with his mouth full, put his elbows on the table, and spill his food, winning handily. Dottie upped the stakes by creating a new Mr. Manners out of pipe cleaners to be worn to school on the jacket of the chief offender. Unfazed, David boasted to his friends about how he'd earned Mr. Manners in spirited competition, then gave them tips on winning one too.

Though David proved to be a good student, he encountered his first conspicuous failure in kindergarten, when he discovered he was the only kid who couldn't tie his shoelaces. Fortunately, two compassionate girls — Lisa and Laura — came to his aid each day after nap period. David was beyond such benign intervention in first grade when the same lack of physical dexterity earned him an F in printing, then in penmanship and in art. As an adult, he developed a fine artistic sensibility, but his drawing skills never progressed beyond stick figures. Except for penguins. For reasons unknown, he practised these until he was proficient, years later proudly illustrating a homemade book, *Frederick the Penguin*, with the help of our younger daughters.

Both Dick and Dottie were community leaders and philanthropists. Dick chaired the boards of directors of the Boys and Girls Home and of Goodwill Industries, as well as serving on the board of St. Luke's Hospital. He was also highly respected in his profession, and made the cover of *Money Magazine* as one of America's top ten investment advisors. Dick had an easier rapport with his sons, especially David, than with his daughters. Dick loved to talk business and stocks, and David was right in there with him. People often marvelled at all the facts and figures David could hold in his head — something he inherited, along with his business sense, from his father, though Dick didn't display his knowledge in the same extroverted way.

Dottie was one of the first women to be elected to the Sioux City School Board, where she served two terms. She believed in educating the whole child through contact with nature and the arts, and established a program to combat juvenile delinquency as a member of the Northwest

Iowa Crime Commission. She was also a member of the board of directors of St. Luke's Marion Regional Health Center, and co-founded Cancervivors, a cancer peer support program. When she was in her fifties, she earned a second bachelor degree in fine arts, then launched herself as a painter. At age sixty-five, she became an Episcopal deacon, affirming decades of work in the community with the sick and disadvantaged. From her early years, Dottie felt called to service, and she taught her children that, whether as a vocation or as a volunteer, serving your community is something that you do.

Ancestors were also an important part of growing up a Pecaut. David's great-great-grandfather Gustav was a fur trader of Swiss-French descent, who, at age fourteen and penniless, immigrated to America with his older sister. According to family lore, the two of them had run away from a cruel stepmother. While the sister stayed in New York, Gustav pushed westward. This was in the early 1850s. At first, Gustav settled on the lower side of the Missouri River in Nebraska, where he became one of the first deed holders. Then, while rafting on the Missouri River, his craft became stuck, forcing him to spend the winter on the Sioux City side. He decided to stay, becoming the third white man to settle there.

It was a rough, tough time in America — the wild west of legend. Though Gustav learned the Lakota language to trade with tribes along the Missouri, he reportedly received a few arrows in the back when transactions went awry. He also routinely used a gun to defend his land from squatters. Even today, Pecaut & Company occasionally receives calls from attorneys attempting to sort out deeds with Gustav's name on them. A framed certificate for the Sioux City Columbus Railroad, a Gustav investment, hangs on the company's wall. The collapse of this railroad inspired David to observe, "You can be generally right but specifically wrong," meaning Gustav had been generally right in betting railroads would be the next big thing, but specifically wrong in picking the Sioux City Columbus line. David loved that pithy bit of wisdom, and frequently referred to it in his speeches. He would have been delighted to know that our youngest daughter, Becca, quoted and illustrated that concept in the personal essay that was part of her application to a number of American universities, all of which accepted her.

Dottie's ancestors were also pioneers with their share of colourful characters. Her spunky mother, Dorothy, who grew up on a Montana ranch, was an excellent horsewoman and apparently a sure shot with a rifle. As the story goes, young Dorothy was playing outside when her mother suddenly yelled at her to stay still. When Dorothy looked up, she saw her mother aiming a rifle at her, and thought she was about to be punished for doing something bad. Her mother fired, killing, with one perfect shot, the rattlesnake poised to attack her daughter.

Dottie's father, Sidney Kent, was a hardscrabble surveyor for the National Parks Service, then later worked his way up from a salesman at Prudential Insurance to vice-president. His drive to achieve and succeed was something he instilled in his own family. When David and Dan were ten and eleven, Grandpa Sid (called Grund by his grandchildren) was in his late sixties, and challenged them to a basketball contest. To their dismay, he sank ten out of ten baskets from the free throw line, then told the boys, "Don't come into the house until you can make eleven out of ten!" That became a family saying: eleven out of ten.

David's sister Shelley explained, "For most people, eleven out of ten would represent the impossible. Years later, while shooting hoops with David in the driveway, we pondered how we could achieve that." The Pecaut children decided it would not be cheating if a person could sink eleven balls with ten tosses. "If we could toss two balls with one arm movement and calibrate the trajectories so that one ball swished and the other hit the back board and bounced in ... it could be done! While we never achieved it, we realized that eleven out of ten could not only be possible — heck, twenty out of ten might be achievable!"

Grund liked to tell stories that had a moral ending. Dick, on the other hand, enjoyed telling jokes. He repeated the same jokes over and over, amidst protesting groans, but he would laugh so hard himself that everyone ended up laughing too. Though a gifted storyteller, David did not inherit the paternal joke gene. He would elaborate, extrapolate, and exaggerate so much it would throw off the punch line, provided he could even remember what that was. Usually, he'd stop in the middle to ask me, "How did that go again?" so I ended up taking on Dick's mantle in our own family as the joke teller, while David reigned supreme as the storyteller.

It was also Grund who inspired his grandchildren with his own love of nature. Starting when David was about four, the Pecauts would join the Kents, including Dottie's sisters and their families, at the Dairymen's Country Club, a nature preserve in northern Wisconsin, for what became a summer rite — fishing, hiking, playing golf and tennis. A generation later, some of our own family's happiest vacations were in those same cabins that David had known as a kid.

As the Pecaut children matured, street life became important in defining who they were. Every day after school, the neighbourhood kids played sports according to the season. Basketball was part of David's being, an all-year favourite, sometimes played in the snow wearing big black boots. One summer, inspired by a stopwatch their mother had given them, David and Dan set up the Valley Drive Olympics, using lawn chairs as hurdles. When the big guys finally allowed David to join in their football games, he was so thrilled that the joy of inclusion became engraved on his heart as a life lesson. Being short often put David at a disadvantage, but diligent practice and smart playing allowed him to compete against more formidable players. He came to relish the role of the underdog who manages to win against the odds, giving him the confidence to tackle challenges in which he lacked a natural advantage.

Charlie, the Pecauts' pet pug, was an important family member. David insisted that his ears smelled like muffins and that all the kids on the street wanted to sniff them. To celebrate Charlie's birthday, David recalled his sisters inviting the neighbourhood dogs for a canine festival, then making up games for them to play. It was a huge success until things got out of hand and Dottie ordered everyone out of the house. One big poodle became so hyper that he dragged his hapless owner around the front yard.

Given how much David adored Charlie, it was puzzling that he never bonded with *our* family dogs, whom he merely tolerated. Then Dan explained: Charlie wasn't a dog: he and David had attributed mystical status to him as an old soul whom he later compared to Yoda.

The adults on Valley Drive got together for regular potluck dinners, and their families even took weekend trips together. When the mother of a local boy wouldn't let him keep his bug collection indoors, Dottie let him store it in her freezer. This, as it turned out, was a contribution to NASA research, since Timmy's high school bug proposal would later be chosen to be conducted in space. Dottie was that kind of mother, Valley Drive was that kind of neighbourhood, and Sioux City was that kind of hometown.

David was a born entrepreneur. He earned money delivering papers, mowing lawns, washing cars, making T-shirts, and selling anything he could lay his hands on — lemonade, castoff toys, and the Christmas cards advertised in the back of comic books. These came in boxes of forty that he divided with Dan and peddled door to door. David sold his in a day or two, but weeks later Dan still had not sold any, and the card company was hounding them for the money.

At Dottie's request, David accompanied his brother to the first house. He heard Dan's shy request: "You wouldn't want these Christmas cards, would you?"

Customer: "Well, I might. Can I see them?"

"Sure. I guess."

"They look really nice. Maybe I'll buy two boxes."

Dan, amazed: "You will?"

David and his dad teased Dan after that, predicting that he was not destined for a career in sales. Ironically, it was Dan who became a partner in Pecaut & Company, where he proved himself an excellent salesman and investment advisor, modelling himself on Warren Buffett's philosophy of value investing.

By the time David was twelve, he was an avid reader of magazines and newspapers, at first the sports section of the *Des Moines Register*, later politics and the stock market. Initially, this was an attempt to reach out to his father, who could usually be found in his La-Z-Boy recliner in front of the TV with a stack of papers, in his own comfortable world. David certainly succeeded in capturing his father's attention when he told him that he wanted to invest the $200 he'd saved, because he understood that money could make money. Dick took David to the Pecaut & Company office and showed him the annual reports of five companies, then told him to choose. David picked Brunswick Corporation, a maker of boats and bowling balls, because his friends loved to bowl. Decades later, at Dick's retirement party, David discovered Brunswick was still in business and that he had made about 8 percent a year for forty years!

One of David's entrepreneurial projects struck Dan with awe, then provided him, much later, with a sibling's inadvertent revenge. It was summer, and the street gang was looking for something to do. David hatched the idea of making a movie.

Cheers all around.

Since the gang was enamoured of TV shows like *Hogan's Heroes* and *Rat Patrol,* it was obvious that this should be a war movie, for which they already had an arsenal of plastic swords and guns for props.

As excitement escalated, it dawned on the movie moguls, "We don't have a camera."

Dan was goggle-eyed at David's nonchalant reply, "Oh, I can get that." Though Dan knew his father had a Super-8, only his parents were allowed to touch it.

The gang created a whiteboard, featuring a title with crossed swords and a helmet.

Another stumbling block: "We don't have any film!"

David had that one covered, too. At age twelve, he was about to state one of the great principles of capitalism: "We'll sell tickets, then use the money to buy the film." Ergo, use other people's money for venture financing.

David went door to door, boasting about the masterwork to come and pre-selling tickets at twenty-five cents apiece. After that, he *did* manage to get a camera — Dan doesn't remember how. They shot the title and an opening battle sequence in the woods with clods of earth as ammunition. *What next?* Interest flagged. The basketball came out. The film was never finished, and the investors' money was never refunded.

Decades later, when David was starting up a high-risk e-commerce company in New York, reporters phoned Dan for background colour. This anecdote, demonstrating David's ability to talk people out of their money without refunding or producing, was not the best introduction to the Fortune 500 clients David hoped to impress.

Even in elementary school, David demonstrated a zeal for organizing. In Grade 6, the lack of an inter-school sports league struck him as a terrible deprivation. He went from school to school, signing up football teams for a weekend round robin and generating a great deal of enthusiasm. Then came the call to the principal's office. Nicely but firmly, she explained, "You can't hold your tournament. The school's insurance won't allow for it."

Of course, David argued, "Then we won't hold it on the school grounds."

The principal was adamant. "No. The tournament already has our name attached. It cannot happen."

David recalled this as his first crash against a wall of authority, when nothing he said could make any difference.

Most of David's early disappointments involved the sports he loved so much. In Grade 9, he was a pass receiver with the Herbert Hoover Junior High football team. During the season, they'd lost only one game, but for the finals they would be facing their archrival, Hayworth School, whose team had won every game by at least thirty points.

Hoover's coach, Tom Tooey, gave David's team a rousing, if eccentric, pre-game locker room pep talk: "Gentleman, Hayworth has an incredible team. We are clearly the underdogs. If you lose by twenty-five points, people will say, 'Well, what did you expect?' If you lose by only ten points, everyone will say, 'Wow! That was good.' Gentlemen, if you go out on that field today and win, no one in the state of Iowa will ever forget you."

David's team was so pumped they thought they could walk on water. Alas, superior strength and skill still counted for something. They were creamed, at something like fifty to zero, providing a tough dose of reality: Yes, faith can move mountains, but sometimes the mountains win.

Though David still believed he could become a professional athlete if only he practised hard enough, his tenth-grade football coach advised him, "Pecaut, I know you put a lot into the team, but you should invest your time where it counts. I'm told you're good at debating, and our practices conflict with that. Why don't you follow your strengths?"

At age fifteen, David's dream of becoming a basketball star was dashed even more decisively. At Iowa State University basketball camp, where his parents enrolled him and Dan for a week, each boy was to receive a session of assessment and advice from legendary coach Maury John of Drake University. When David's turn came, John told him, "You're a great ball-handler and strategic player. You know how to hustle, and you get a lot of baskets." Then came the kicker: "How tall are you?"

David never made it past five-foot-eight, maybe five-foot-eight-and-a-half on a generous day.

"When was the last time you had a growth spurt?"

Once again, David's response was not promising.

"Do you have any other sports?"

David perked up. "I run track and cross-country, maybe five or six miles a day."

"Great, that's where you can really shine," enthused Coach John as David's face fell.

David did astound the camp's coaches with a special ability. In one drill, each player was supposed to bounce two balls against the wall for as long as possible. The record was 30 bounces; David's score was 120.

David also provided a brotherly service for Dan, who was being picked on by an older, bigger kid in his classroom.

"Don't worry, I'll take care of it," David assured Dan, and he did. He confronted the bully with three of his buddies — no doubt with a skilful tongue-lashing rather than anything Soprano-style. The bully transferred rooms, and Dan couldn't have been more grateful.

The coaches who punctured David's dream of becoming a sports star actually gave him excellent advice. He became a champion cross-country runner who loved to compete and who took this talent into his adult life. Typically, Dan followed his brother into the sport, but whereas David ran full out then threw up after every race, Dan listened to his body, slowed down when he felt like it, and was happy to stay with the pack. As he explained, "I thought it was cool to have such a talented brother, but I didn't feel any pressure to compete."

David also became a champion high school debater, a training that honed his natural talent for marshalling, structuring, and synthesizing facts. He and his debating partner, Rich Levy, won a string of debates in Iowa, Minnesota, and South Dakota, and emerged as lifelong friends. According to Rich, David was particularly adept at taking the opposition apart, even when he didn't have the evidence. "One round, he read from a note card that was totally unfamiliar to me, and seemed to eviscerate the opposition. I was amazed. Afterwards, I asked to see the card. It was blank. He'd invented it on the spot. My hero."

Rich, who had recently relocated from a Jewish neighbourhood in Chicago, had found Sioux City (Herbert Hoover Junior High in particular) a severe cultural shock. David and the Pecaut family warmly welcomed him into what was essentially a white-bread culture. In exchange, Rich introduced David to his Jewish heritage, represented by lox, bagels, kugel, and chicken soup. While David was on his cross-country marathons, he would sometimes stop at the Levy home, continuing to run on the spot while talking to Rich's mother, who made it clear that he was the only gentile she would allow to marry her daughter, Ellen. In fact, everyone's parents liked David because he was always the designated driver who piled their drunken kids into his car after a rowdy party and literally rolled them home.

The Pecauts were a politically aware family with members espousing independent views. Though Dottie was once a "Goldwater Girl" Republican, she became an independent voter, often voting differently from Dick. Dan became a Republican, and Stacey and Shelley became Democrats, as did David.

In junior high, David experimented with politics by running for president of the student council against his friend Rick Wagner. David was a good student, involved in sports and the school newspaper — an idea man. Rick was football quarterback and centre of the basketball team. Even David's friends were predicting that Rick would win in a landslide.

After a boisterous buildup that included posters and rallies, the campaign was to climax with a big speech in front of the student body. Knowing that words were his strength, David devised a bold platform that involved raising money through events like bake sales to install lockers and to buy bleachers for the football field so fans wouldn't have to stand. He finished to polite applause.

His opponent took the podium. "I'm Rick Wagner."

Everyone cheered.

"I want to be your president."

More cheering.

"I like what David said, so if I'm elected, I'll get David's help, and we'll do all those things."

Thunderous applause.

The principal broke the results of the election to the candidates in private: Rick had won, as expected. Since the principal wouldn't reveal the count even when David insisted, he concluded it had been another Hayworth versus Hoover rout. As Rick had promised, he appointed David to do everything David had suggested. And David did, despite being rankled by the unfairness, which he blamed on the immaturity of voters too easily swayed by popularity. He felt it would have been sounder to elect a council, then to let that council choose its own officers.

This story has a sweet dénouement. For Grade 12, David moved from Central High to a newly created school, West High. He was asked, as an acknowledged big thinker, to draft a student constitution — his first opportunity to set public policy. Over the summer, he designed a system stipulating that an elected council would choose its own officers. In the fall, his constitution was accepted. David was elected as a grade rep, and then the council chose him as president.

David and his debating partner, Rich Levy, celebrated their graduation from high school in 1973 with a summer road trip. Though the Levys had by then returned to Chicago, the friends had kept in touch. Rich had never been camping — the beginning of David's belief, projected onto me, that Jews didn't camp — so David showered him with advice and equipment lists.

In June, the two of them set out in Dick and Dottie's burnt orange Datsun 210, with gas at only thirty cents a gallon, in search of adventure. For almost eight weeks, they hiked and climbed the mountains of Colorado, Utah, and Wyoming. They camped everywhere, using tube tents whenever it rained. They grew beards and long hair, played guitar, shared poetry, and kept journals. Nearly every night, they saw shooting stars.

One campfire ritual must have been unique. As a kid, David had had his mouth washed out with soap for saying, "Goddammit!" As an accomplished Boy Scout with the badges to prove it, he had settled on his own pseudo curse — "Oh, crash!" — to express extremes of frustration. Now, as a male rite of passage, Rich taught David to use the expletives scrawled on washroom walls with satisfying conviction.

David also credited Rich with a second act of liberation. Whenever they went grocery shopping, David would always defer: "Whatever you want is fine with me." Rich challenged him into admitting that he *did* have preferences, while persuading him that being too eager to please was not a recipe for future happiness. On the other hand, David became angry at Rich — their only quarrel — for putting American flag stamps upside down on his postcards to protest American involvement in Vietnam. Apparently neither of them knew this was also the way lovers communicated their feelings for the recipient.

As Rich summed up this magical, footloose summer, "We spoke of our dreams, our hopes, of college, women, books, music. We talked about our future, the mountains, our families, our fears. We even had a secret word, which we never stopped using. On this trip, we became brothers."

David's childhood was rich with the qualities he would bring to his adult life: a love of family, irrepressible curiosity, a passion for risk, a quick tongue backed by a quicksilver mind, a compassion for the underdog, a powerful sense of community, an ability to charm, never-ending resourcefulness, and a reliable moral compass.

As Dan irreverently expressed it, the Pecaut siblings were members of "the lucky sperm club," and all proved generous in using their inherited good fortune on behalf of others.

David was not without his flaws. Like his father, David sometimes had an angry, impatient temper that he had to learn to control, especially when he himself became a parent. The outburst that David would most regret occurred when Amy was about fourteen. She and her friends had been out well past their curfew. All of us parents had been trying to contact our kids on their pagers (this was pre cellphones), then calling each other when we failed to get answers. Finally, Amy and a bunch turned up at our place. All claimed their pagers were either broken or had been stolen. David, furious with worry, tore into them, angered as much by the stupidity of their excuses as by their lateness. We had always tried to turn our home into a sanctuary for our daughters and their friends, and now most were afraid to return. Amy's response — that David had a right to bawl her out, but not to yell at her companions — seemed reasonable to him, and he made a real effort after that at anger management.

More problematic, David loved the limelight and all the praise that went with it. When the Pecaut kids arrived home from school, both parents would ask, "What did you do today?" David would start in on his exploits and go on and on, and when he was finished, no one else had anything to say. If ever David felt overshadowed in his family, he would drop out of the competition. Both of his parents were terrific golfers, and his sisters were formidable contenders in the state tennis doubles championships. David was the only one in the family who was not a skilful tennis player, and he didn't keep up his golf. His siblings grew up with the feeling that their parents favoured David, and this was not a family of shrinking violets. All are accomplished: Dan, an investment advisor who writes a thoughtful and witty newsletter; Shelley, now a writer in Geneva after a successful international development career; and Stacey, an Episcopal priest and head chaplain in the Sioux City hospital where all the Pecaut kids were born. Nevertheless, it was David who had his confidence reinforced at every turn. He grew up with the idea, "You're the best, you're the brightest," and that became a need.

As I came to understand the Pecaut family dynamic, they often divided into fast and slow talkers. David, his father, and his sisters were the fast talkers; his mother and brother were slower talkers. They were just as smart, but if you asked them a question, they'd say, "Well ...," and in that pause David would have three arguments ready and take control of the conversation.

As he himself later admitted, "I took up a lot of space in my family."

CHAPTER FOUR

The Harvard Years

Dick and Dottie drove David cross-country from Sioux City to Harvard University — what parents did for their seventeen-year-old kids in 1973.

They couldn't have been prouder. When David was fourteen, he had told his father, "I read an article that says Harvard is the best university in the world. I'd like to go there." Dick had replied, "It's hard to get in, but if you can make it, I'll support you." He thought he'd heard the last of this, until a Harvard catalogue arrived in the mail.

David, who had graduated from high school as a National Merit Scholar, applied to Harvard, Yale, and Stanford, and was accepted at all three. He chose Harvard.

For the kid from Sioux City, encountering a big city like Boston was a thrill. He'd never before seen a subway. Even escalators — something they didn't have in Sioux City — excited him.

Harvard itself was like "a great big candy store," bursting with inspiring ideas and unimagined opportunities. He loved the dynamic convergence of brilliant minds. He loved the variety, breadth, and depth of the courses on offer — music, philosophy, sociology, theology, physics. Of course, he joined the debating club and signed up for running and track. Yet, true to his Sioux City and Pecaut family roots, he also volunteered during his first week on campus to work in a drop-in centre at an East Boston housing project with a large minority population. He also became a Big Brother to a boy whom he took to baseball games and came to love.

David radiated such incredible energy! John Paul MacDuffie and Lloyd David, his college roommates and lifelong friends, remember his habit of vaulting over parking meters, without warning or fanfare, sometimes in mid-conversation, as they walked down the street. Leaping became a David signature. After he finished a consulting project he would jump up to touch the ceiling as if on springs. He loved being airborne.

John Paul and Lloyd remember games of touch football — except, of course, David had converted the sport into something he called Razzle Dazzle. Usually he was the quarterback, calling plays so elaborate that it took Harvard minds to follow them.

Even at Harvard, David's prismatic intellect, grasp of ideas, virtuoso way with a story, and erudite vocabulary stood out. John Paul, nocturnal like David, remembers conversational orgies lasting into the wee hours; he admired how his friend merged flashes of ideas seamlessly into an ongoing flow, perhaps interrupted by a pinball game at Tommy's Lunch. Lloyd remembers becoming charmed enough by David to overlook his first negative impression: David, at a party, proclaiming in a phony British accent with paragraphs punctuated by "Cheerio!"

In David's sophomore year, he decided to major in sociology because it was a new department, with thirty faculty members to only thirty students. It also had the fewest course requirements, allowing for a plethora of possibilities leading to what would essentially be an arts degree. In one philosophy course, David became caught up in the vigorous centuries-old debate pitting free will against determinism. Though he was emotionally attached to free will, he found the determinist arguments depressingly compelling. At year's end, David decided to ignore the exam questions and to spend the three hours writing an essay explaining that he was predetermined to do this, thereby confronting his professors with the same dilemma he was experiencing. In a grand rush of conviction, he ended his essay with a dare: "To give me an A or an F would be appropriate, but to give me a C would be a copout."

David's essay caused the commotion he had anticipated. One professor wanted to give him an A; the other, an F. A third was brought in to arbitrate. David didn't receive his grade until the end of the summer: B-plus.

His brother, Dan, and two other newly minted freshmen drove David cross-country for his junior year. David, who was suffering from mononucleosis, spent much of the time stretched out on a couch in the rear of their U-haul. Once back on campus, resting was certainly not on his agenda. He plunged right in as usual.

Because Harvard offered such a feast of activities, the brothers had to make formal plans to meet for dinner or a concert. In David's freshman year, he discovered Boston's jazz clubs — an enthusiasm he passed on to Dan. He then took his passion to another level by designing a Harvard non-degree course to teach others how to listen to music. He also created a jazz program for WHRB, Harvard's student radio station. John Paul had a classical program, and they cooperated at the end of each semester to fill reading periods with obsessive, around-the-clock marathons featuring a particular musician, composer, or theme. John Paul remembers engineering for David during a thirty-hour show featuring jazz pianist Thelonious Monk. He also compared David's conversational style to that of a great jazz improviser — building from core riffs, always with a sense of structure, yet offering something unique and fresh, a creation of the moment. Many years later, one of David's business colleagues coincidentally chose jazz as a metaphor for his consulting style — unpredictable, spontaneous, wide-ranging, without obvious structure, but always taking the conversation where it needed to go.

David played the piano — his favourite instrument — in the same unscripted way. He wasn't a great reader of music, despite Dottie's early insistence on piano lessons, and he didn't like to play other people's compositions. To use John Paul's description once again, he preferred to doodle away, making up melodies, often beginning with a simple motif, sometimes elaborated with intense repetition or dramatic changes of tempo and swelling crescendos, often reaching a nearly meditative state. In confirmation of philosopher Heraclitus's reflection on time — that you can never enter the same river twice — David never played any piece exactly the same way. To him, music was unpredictable because it was alive.

For his third and fourth years at Harvard, David lived with John Paul and Lloyd in Dunster House, a university residence. His exuberance over the most mundane of tasks was infectious. Even his fledgling efforts at cooking were celebrated by him in the most exalted of terms. He made the *best* chocolate chip cookies. He made the *best* hamburgers. As John Paul and Lloyd later deadpanned by way of a reality check, "Well, they were pretty good."

The roommates spoke candidly about their girlfriends, their hopes, and their evolving philosophies. Yet both Lloyd and John Paul believe David's most compelling dialogues must have taken place with his professors as he negotiated extensions on his term papers. For an assignment due on May 26, he would wrangle a June 10 deadline, then maybe push that to midsummer. A distraught Dottie would sometimes discover that David was finishing his last semester's projects when due to return for another year.

———————

Like many university students, David lived a dual life — academic elitist in winter, body-for-hire in summer.

Between his freshman and sophomore years, he applied for a construction job requiring him to turn up at a union hiring office at 6:00 a.m. Since the lineup was already too long, he returned the second day at 5:00 a.m. After waiting till 8:00, he was told there were no jobs. The same thing happened on the third day. Figuring something fishy might be going on, David hung around till 10:00. Sure enough, a guy walked in off the street and was immediately assigned a job. When David questioned the hiring official, he was told the ten o'clock guy's uncle was in the union. Though David generally felt positive about unions, he was indignant at this unfairness, and wanted to write an editorial exposing the practice. His father dissuaded him: "Don't be crazy. Those men are tough."

David found a job pumping gas at a riverside marina and helping with emergency rescues. He had a terrific summer.

Between his sophomore and junior years, David worked at an Iowa meat packing plant. His job — to clean up fat trimmed off assembly-line cattle carcasses — was the lowliest in the company. At the start of his shift, the temperature was near freezing in order to kill bacteria. For that same reason, steam was then pumped in to raise the temperature to around 120° F. He and his crew would start out in winter clothes, then strip down to boots and shorts. The floors were precipitously slippery, and the chemicals they used, such as aluminum chloride, were dangerous. The worst part of cleanup was when he and his crew were ordered to climb thirty-foot ladders to squeegee the bacteria-laden condensation from the metal bars of the ceiling.

One morning, David's crew, including his foreman, were replaced by senior workers. A government inspection had been scheduled. Afterward, the company was fined several hundred dollars, and David's foreman never returned.

David sometimes had to raise two-hundred-pound barrels of offal on a forklift, then pour each load into a vat. If he missed, he would have to scrub up the offal splashed across the floor. On learning this was supposed to be a two-person job, he asked his boss why he was treating him so sadistically. The boss replied, "I saw you were from Harvard, and I wanted to get rid of you." Eventually, the boss relented and gave David a helper.

Safety and sanitary conditions were not stringently enforced. When David accidentally contaminated a couple dozen boxes of T-bone steaks by poking them through with his forklift, he was told to load them backward on the truck to conceal the damage. Though he was assured they would be discarded on arrival, he felt guilt-ridden.

Some of David's co-workers were Mexicans who couldn't speak English. He, at least, had the option of registering a complaint with the union. The grievance officer showed him a spindle stacked with files. "See this? Yours is going right at the bottom. When we sit down with the company, they'll say, 'Give us ten out of the first one hundred. If you try to push for more, we'll take every single one to court.' We would rather get lucky with ten than lose them all."

When David reported these incidents in disgust to Dick, his father told him, "That's why you're going to Harvard. So you don't have to put up with these injustices."

In 2001, David read *Fast Food Nation: The Dark Side of the All-American Meal*, by investigative journalist Eric Schlosser. He discovered the chapter indicting the meat-processing industry was focused on the same plant where he had worked. David's first-hand experience of the class system while employed there later informed his civic work and passion for social justice.

During David's third year at Harvard, he began musing to his close friends, "Wouldn't it be great if we could find some profitable way of spending the summer together instead of going home to work?" With David, the thought was always close to the deed, so it surprised no one when he found a group project that he even managed to turn into his senior sociology thesis.

Just as David liked to compose his own music, he wanted to do original research instead of merely regurgitating other people's ideas. He applied for, and received, a $12,000 National Science Foundation grant, becoming the first undergraduate in the social sciences to do so. His intent was to dispute a thesis, advanced by Herbert Gans in *The Urban Villagers*, that low-income groups did not have the capacity for effective political organization. Gans's findings had been based on the inability of residents of a west-end Boston community to mobilize to prevent the expansion of a downtown expressway. David based his counter thesis on the fact that residents of East Boston, a poor Italian community where he had volunteered, had dramatically mobilized thousands of people on two occasions: first, in a right-wing attempt to stop court-ordered school busing intended to end segregation; second, in a left-wing attempt to stop Boston's Logan International Airport from encroaching on their community through the addition of another runway.

Using his grant, David employed five friends, including John Paul and Lloyd, to spend the summer studying East Boston. They rented an apartment in a tenement, where they were the only non-Italians, then immersed themselves in the local culture.

By interviewing a random sampling of the seventy thousand residents, then circulating a questionnaire among their leaders, David's team learned that effective mobilization depended on two things: the immediacy and degree of the threatened impact and what Professor Mark Granovetter had labelled "the strength of weak ties."

In sociology, "strong ties" refers to the linkage among relatives or close friends; "weak ties" describes the linkage among people who normally come into contact during an ordinary day or week, such as shoppers with their local butcher or parents with their child's teacher. Since strong ties are necessarily limited in number, weak ties provide the glue for broad-scale organizing. In East Boston, the airport protest came out of church basements led by leftist Roman Catholic priests, while the anti-busing protest emerged out of a network of bowling leagues. As David explained, "People would turn up for bowling, and they'd hear, 'We're going to lock down the federal court building,' and eight hundred bowlers and their friends might turn up."

Though only the airport protest succeeded, both mobilized large numbers to their cause. While interviewing, often face-to-face across a kitchen table, the Harvard friends learned intimate, sometimes unexpected facts about a culture different from their own. For example, some of the busing opposition was racist, as anticipated, but some expressed the residents' poignant concern about the stress placed on their commuting children and the breakup of their neighbourhood.

David's faculty advisor commended his team for their graduate-level research, sophisticated enough for a Ph.D. dissertation. Decades later, David would attribute some of his success with the Toronto City Summit Alliance to the knowledge he acquired that summer: "I learned going all the way back to my senior thesis on East Boston that the power of networks is often the most important unseen hand in the local economy. Weak tie networks are at the root of social mobilization, particularly in communities and cities, and every addition to the network has a multiplier effect, just as in telecommunications."

In David's final year, he applied for a Shaw Fellowship, granting the winner a year's travel in Europe while field-researching his or her proposal. So did John Paul. Both were from the same department, they had letters of recommendation from the same advisors, and neither had ever been outside of the United States. As John Paul tells the story, one afternoon he walked into their shared quarters to the high-volume sound of a jet engine revving up — the introduction to the Beatles' "Back in the U.S.S.R." Friends jumped out from behind furniture, shouting congratulations. David had taken the phone call confirming that John Paul had won the Shaw. After what was likely a few seconds of disappointment, David identified so completely with his friend's success that he organized this spontaneous celebration.

Later, at the Class of '77's big graduation party in Dunster House, David listened as his friends announced, one by one, plans to pursue a post-graduate degree, enter a family business, or test their talents in the arts. When his turn came, he reported that he was considering becoming a long-haul trucker or a radio disc jockey. He was serious.

David left Harvard with glowing memories and a sense of boundless opportunity. He had met some of the finest minds in the world and made the best friends of his life — people with whom he kept in close contact and whose children became like cousins to our children. A follow-up study of his Harvard class found that its members chose the same types of professions as other grads and accumulated the same level of wealth, yet remained more liberal and socially active. David both contributed to that attitude and was its beneficiary.

The "three amigos" — John Paul, Lloyd, and David — celebrated their college graduation the same way David had celebrated his final year of high school, with a road trip across the United States, camping under the stars. At David's suggestion, they began each morning with a wonderful ritual. To squeeze the air out of their tents for packing, they put the tents between themselves, then exchanged a big bear hug — a grownup version of little brothers throwing kisses.

CHAPTER FIVE

Fertilizer, Finance, and Fine Arts

I n the fall of 1977, David made his most important sales pitch to date. It went something like this: "I have a great background. I can learn anything quickly. I want to spend a year working with you, but not as your secretary. I want to be your executive assistant to deal with any problems you want. I'm cheap, and at the end of the year, I'm gone. I'll exit sooner, no complaint, if this doesn't work."

After striking out in an attempt to parlay his Harvard bachelor degree, *summa cum laude*, into a job as a long-haul trucker or a radio disc jockey, David combined two good ideas: to return to Sioux City, where he knew the environment, and to apprentice himself to a business leader for a year to see how a major American corporation functioned.

He had already been turned down by CEOs of two of the Midwest's biggest companies, who essentially said, "I have these boxes to fill and you don't fit.'"

The third CEO — William Dible, head of Terra Chemicals International, a Fortune 1000 fertilizer company — was enthusiastic. He offered David an invented job as Special Projects Administrator, a big title carrying a humble salary of $1,000 a month. This was fine with David, because he was living at home, and the title carried with it the privilege of walking into any employee's office and asking what he or she did. Priceless.

With characteristic zeal, David began learning everything about the fertilizer business. He also followed the advice he would later give to young consultants: Find out when the boss takes some quiet time, then make yourself available for conversations that will build a relationship. With Dible, this was Saturday mornings, from eight till one. David made a point of turning up, while being careful not to threaten other employees by assuring them he was leaving after a year.

As proof that confidence had indeed been established, Dible assigned his Special Projects Administrator his biggest challenge: to represent Terra in Washington at a Senate hearing aimed at stopping Russia from dumping below-cost ammonia fertilizer in the U.S. At twenty-three, David was half the age of other company reps, who kept asking, "Hey, kid, where's your boss?" Then, in a meeting with Senator Bob Dole, he received his first taste of old-style Washington politics when the senator began by asking, "Now, has everybody here contributed to my political action committee?"

David's SOS call to Dible received a brisk, "No, we haven't, and don't get sucked into that!"

On his return to Sioux City, David submitted a report that earned him a succinct, "Great job." There was only one problem: his expense account.

"What's this?" demanded Dible. "You were in Washington four days and you spent $23? Where did you sleep?"

"At a friend's place."

"Where did you eat?"

"At McDonald's."

"What about taxis?"

"I walked."

"Look, this is a business trip. You're entitled to stay in a decent hotel, eat decent meals, and take taxis."

It was at Terra that David was introduced to the world of consulting.

Dible had invited a team from the global firm McKinsey & Company to review Terra's manufacturing strategy. When David encountered a stranger only a few years older in Terra's washroom, he asked, "What project are you working on?

"I'm with McKinsey."

"Oh, how long have you been in the fertilizer industry?"

"I haven't."

"But you *do* know that Terra is looking for a manufacturing strategy? Haven't you done any work on nitrogen fertilizers?"

"No."

David went directly to Dible to wise him up. "I think you're being taken for a ride, Bill. This guy from McKinsey doesn't know anything about fertilizers."

"That's okay," assured Dible. "These consultants have a methodology for gathering facts. They'll figure things out."

As David watched the consulting process unfold, he became less skeptical; however, he still had a final question for Dible: "Did you really learn anything new? I can't believe that you didn't already know the answers they gave you."

Dible confirmed, "I felt intuitively that the path they recommended was right for the company, but it was a controversial decision with my board, and it also meant firing the head of manufacturing. I needed more clarity, for *my* sake as well as for the board's."

David was impressed with this reasoning. He also thought it would be fun to go from company to company, learning everything you could in a few weeks or a few months, then moving on. Here was a career that just might counter his low boredom threshold. At the same time, Dible was encouraging David to get to know the First Boston investment bankers, with whom he himself had a close relationship. As a result, David ended his apprenticeship with a career choice that bounced between Wall Street and consulting.

But David found yet another option: On graduation from Harvard, he had deferred a Rotary fellowship for a one-year degree in philosophy in order to gain some real-life experience. Maybe, after all, he might like to be a professor?

David chose Sussex University in Brighton, England, because it, like Harvard, was open to interdisciplinary study and because it had become a haven for Oxford and Cambridge scholars who also chafed under traditional academic restraints. As usual, his course of study was offbeat. He combined philosophy with music, based on the curriculum he had designed at Harvard — a choice that couldn't have been further from finance and fertilizer.

David wrote his master's thesis on philosopher Theodore Adorno, who asked such probing questions as: Does music have meaning? If so, how does an artistic medium like music convey its meaning? He was grateful that his father supported what other practical-minded fathers might have considered a year of dalliance. However, all this nonstop abstract talk began to feel surreal. Though he loved Sussex, he became convinced that the academic world moved too slowly to satisfy his need for stimulation and action.

———————

David returned to Sioux City in 1979. His mother had been diagnosed with late-stage histiocytic lymphoma, and David wished to help — if not lead — the nursing team. He also needed to finish his thesis.

By the fall of 1980, Dottie had finished an aggressive round of chemotherapy treatments in Madison, Wisconsin. This involved an experimental cocktail of five drugs administered in massive doses. Miraculously, she survived. She returned to Madison for the balance of her punishing treatment regime, which now involved radiation. David and his siblings helped to care for their mother in both Sioux City and Madison. They marvelled at her resilience and ultimate triumph, given the overwhelming odds.

Somehow, David managed to complete his thesis. Though he wanted to hang around Sioux City to monitor his mother's health, he also wanted to get on with his life. He started his own consulting company, Missouri Valley Associates (an exaggeration, since he had no associates). To attract clients, he used a variation of the same pitch he'd used with Bill Dible: "It's true, I have no experience, but if you don't like what I do, you don't have to pay me, so what's your risk?" His first client — no surprise! — was Bill Dible at Terra Chemicals. He also became involved in public policy for economic development with a tri-state team from Iowa, South Dakota, and Nebraska. As he admitted, he was making it up as he went along: "I figured consulting was like plumbing. If you paid attention, you could learn it."

David also talked his way into a non-paying job disc-jockeying a six-and-a-half-hour Saturday night radio program called *Jazz in the Night*,

David and his brother Dan playing basketball with their dad in the driveway of their Valley Drive home in Sioux City, circa 1969.

David running in a high school track meet, circa 1971.

The Pecaut family Christmas photo, circa *1975.*

'Jazz in the night's' all free

By Jean Novotny
Journal staff writer

It's the kind of a deal in which everyone can "swing."

The staff of radio station KWIT gets Saturday nights off.

Dave Pecaut gets his own show.

Siouxlanders get "Jazz in The Night."

And it doesn't really cost anyone anything. Pecaut hosts the show, a regular Saturday night feature on the public radio station on 90.3-FM, for free.

His reward is the chance to play the music he loves — music that he believes is "alive" and "exciting" and deserves to be heard.

He admits that he's "hooked" on the medium — the 22-year-old bachelor is so addicted that he gives up his Saturday nights to spend six and a half hours completely by himself in the tiny trailer that is the station's temporary home.

There, from 7 p.m. Saturdays to 1:30 a.m. Sundays, he spins jazz discs and turns on his listeners to the sound of the improvisational music. His style is relaxed and informal, and he delivers the program notes in a low, "sexy" voice that prompted one female listener to his show on a Boston station where he got his start to call to say she would really like to meet him.

Perhaps that's not an unusual happening in the life of the disc jockey, but he was surprised. Unlike most disc jockeys, he is not out to promote himself or his interests — other than jazz.

He says, "The disc jockey's personal life is not of interest."

There are no jokes or what Pecaut calls "hype" on "Jazz in The Night." He feels that the focus of his show, for which he chose the name, should be on the music.

So the talk is on the music, which he considers sacred, in a sense. He will not sing along with it or talk over it. His philosophy is that the music deserves a lot of thought and

This is his
Saturday night

Dave Pecaut, host of "Jazz in the Night" on Radio Station KWIT, prepares notes for his Saturday night show on the public station. Pecaut donates his time to host the show which is the only regular program on a station in this area. photo by Gary Anderson)

David gets his own radio program, Jazz in the Night. Sioux City Journal, *April 23, 1978.*

David with college roommates, John Paul MacDuffie and Lloyd David, on their post-Harvard hiking expedition.

David with Sarah and Becca, fishing off the dock at Dairymen's, Boulder Junction, Wisconsin, 1995.

Canada Consulting Group partners celebrate their twenty-fifth and BCG's thirty-fifth anniversary at the Design Exchange in Toronto, 1992. L–R front row: Jim Coutts, Carolyn Kearns, Sheelagh Whittaker, Stuart Campbell, Jill Black. L–R back row: David Thompson, Neil Paget, Jerome Redican, David Beatty, Jim Fisher, Jim Milway, David Jolley, David Galloway, David Pecaut.

David and fellow BCG rappers shooting a recruitment video at an offsite meeting, 2004.

David and the BCG basketball team during the annual Bay Street Hoops Tournament, April 2006.

David in the April 1, 2002 edition of Maclean's Magazine, *where he is featured as an e-commerce booster who runs the tech firm iFormation Group and chairs the Canadian E-Business Opportunities Roundtable.*

Prime Minister Chretien congratulates David at the 1996 launch of Career Edge in Toronto. Also pictured: Urban Joseph, first Career Edge chairman, and David Galloway, president and CEO of Torstar Corporation.

David receives the 2005 Canadian Urban Institute Award for City Renewal from David Caplan, Minister of Public Infrastructure Renewal at the annual lunch hosted by David Crombie, CUI's president and CEO.

Members of the Canadian E-Business Opportunities Roundtable with Industry Minister Allan Rock gather for the launch of their 1999 report, Fast Forward — Accelerating Canada's Leadership in the Internet Economy.

David and Tony Gagliano (pictured with Premier Dalton McGuinty) are named 2008 Canadians of the Year by the Canadian Club in recognition of their co-founding of Luminato.

With former British Prime Minister Tony Blair when he addressed the Canadian Club of Toronto at a joint event with the Belinda Stronach Foundation, April 24, 2009.

David receives an honorary degree from Seneca College in 2008.

for public station KWIT. He had a mellow voice with lots of warmth, which he pitched into a lower register to sound really cool and sexy. Already a master of publicity, he even got a T-shirt made for his show.

Certainly, romance was on his mind one night when he made a music tape for his girlfriend, then left his tiny trailer station unattended while it was playing — absolutely forbidden! — to surprise her at the 7/11 where she was working.

After two years in Sioux City, and now assured that his mother was in good health, David felt it was time to leave his hometown in pursuit of greater challenges. He had decided that consulting was what he wanted, but where to practise?

David had enjoyed his year in England, and his girlfriend was from Toronto. Though he had been to Canada only once before — for a one-day fishing trip with his dad — he was ripe for a new adventure in a new city.

CHAPTER SIX

The Green Polyester Suit

When David drove into Toronto in 1981, the city was feeling justly pleased with itself. Jane Jacobs, the American urban guru whom David would come to revere, had not only adopted Toronto as her home but also spearheaded a citizens' protest that effectively prevented the city's midtown ravines from being paved as the Spadina Expressway. For six years, Mayor David Crombie had balanced the interests of those who defined progress as another glass tower with those who saw it as preserving Toronto's heritage. He had been succeeded by John Sewell, a radical champion of downtown neighbourhoods as livable spaces for people, not commuter corridors for cars. Torontonians had just elected Art Eggleton, whose mayoralty would be noted for construction of the Convention Centre, the SkyDome, and the Canadian Broadcasting Centre, but also for the expansion of social housing and new parks.

Since David didn't have a work permit, he had plenty of time to explore the city from his Bathurst and St. Clair apartment. He loved Toronto's ocean-sized lake and its ravines snaking through the urban landscape. He loved the vitality of the downtown core, unlike the blighted centres of so many American cities. He loved Toronto's diversity, fluidity, and political openness, in contrast to the intense lobbying and partisanship of Washington. He was inspired by what he felt to be the absence of a class system based on birth and education, as in Britain, or on wealth, as in America. As someone who enjoyed positioning himself with the underdog, he even liked our famed Canadian inferiority complex, which had us politely apologizing to our southern neighbours for any possible offence.

To pay mounting bills, David's girlfriend signed a contract for David that would allow him to deliver phone books using his one asset — the Dodge Colt he had purchased from a used car dealer in Sioux City. Though he could barely afford a coffee, he discovered a restaurant where he could get a hearty bowl of goulash for $1. For entertainment, he could always hang out for free in the library.

When David did finally get his work permit, allowing him to apply for a consulting job, he knew of only one global company based in Toronto: McKinsey & Company, the firm engaged by Bill Dible. For interview experience, David scheduled appointments with two smaller firms — Woods Gordon and Curry Coopers — to be followed by that critical third interview with McKinsey.

A junior partner at Woods Gordon conducted David's initial interview, beginning with the question, "What do you think of Michael Porter's book?"

David had to admit, "I've never heard of Michael Porter."

His interviewer was nonplussed. "You're a graduate of Harvard, and you don't know *Competitive Strategy*, the landmark work of another Harvard grad?"

This led to an even more damaging admission. "I didn't graduate in business at Harvard." In fact, David had never so much as set foot in the prestigious business school or taken an economics course. "My undergraduate degree is in sociology, and my master's is in music and philosophy." Even David's consulting company, Missouri Valley Associates, seemed irrelevant when he had to admit it was a one-man firm.

David was to be interviewed by a senior partner the next day.

He went directly from Woods Gordon to the University of Toronto library, where he read the Porter book. Porter had, he noted, based his business strategies on the economic theories of Harvard's Michael Spence, whose work David did know.

The next day, David initiated his interview with the senior partner instead of waiting to be quizzed. "Let me present what I did for the U.S. agricultural industry at Missouri Valley Associates, drawing on Michael Porter's five forces framework."

Minutes into David's presentation, the senior partner stopped him. "Aren't you the guy who didn't know who Michael Porter was?"

"I didn't yesterday, but I do now. Frankly, his theories aren't all that complex. They simply describe a framework that I applied."

David received an offer from Woods Gordon, as well as one from Curry Coopers. By then, he'd also heard about Canada Consulting Group, and decided to give them a whirl.

CCG had been founded by a brain trust of Canadians, some of whom had split from American-owned McKinsey. Its founding partners included Jim Coutts, former principal secretary to Prime Minister Pierre Trudeau, and future business leaders David Beatty, David Galloway, Jim Fisher, Jerome Redican, and Neil Paget. McKinsey had tried to freeze the Canadians out of their own market, but the strong political connections of founders like Coutts enabled CCG to acquire work with Crown corporations like the Canadian Broadcasting Corporation. By 1981, CCG was thriving in both the private and public sectors.

David's arrival at CCG's Front Street office was somewhat humbling. The CCG receptionist insisted, "Haven't we met? I'm sure I remember you." David did his best to dissuade her. In fact, he'd flirted with her when he'd delivered their phone books from the back of his Dodge Colt, convinced they'd never meet again.

David had seven successive interviews at Canada Consulting Group, and left feeling deeply excited. This feeling proved mutual. Neil Paget, a senior partner with whom David made a special connection, was especially impressed when he heard that David already had a major client in his pocket: Terra Chemicals. Bill Dible again. He told David, "We're excited by you, and we want you to join us." He presented David with a written offer on the spot.

David told Paget that he still had his McKinsey interview — the one to which he'd been building.

Paget offered a subtle yet sly warning: "I think you may find McKinsey isn't as entrepreneurial as we are about your project."

Motivated by Paget's veiled comment, David decided to sound out his McKinsey recruiter over the phone about the client he considered to be his ace in the hole. As he told the recruiter, "I'll be coming to our interview with a project I'm sure will be of value. It's with Terra Chemicals and Hudson Bay Mining."

The recruiter spelled out his firm's policy: "Consulting associates with McKinsey don't have clients. Only senior partners do. If you come here we'll be happy to introduce you to a senior who will take over that portfolio. We don't encourage client relationships until an associate has been here four or five years."

David had a restless night in which he asked himself, *Why would I go to McKinsey when the CCG people are the real entrepreneurs? Since they walked out of McKinsey, won't they have all the same methodologies?*

He cancelled the McKinsey interview and accepted the CCG offer.

There is a legendary postscript to David's CCG hiring. On his first day, Neil Paget told him, "You know, we have a suit allowance with a top Toronto tailor, Harry Rosen. We'll advance you money on your salary to get two suits."

As David loved to recount, "It took six months before I realized that nobody else at CCG had this suit allowance." It had been initiated as an emergency measure at the sight of David's green polyester suit, with its double seams and flashy paisley lining. When Neil had asked David if he had another suit, he had replied with some pride, "Oh yes, there was a sale in Sioux City. I have a white one just like this hanging in my closet."

––––––––––

Canada Consulting Group more than lived up to David's expectations. One day he might be advising government, the next day it might be manufacturers, then maybe bankers after that. But it was the opportunity to work on public policy, an area that deeply interested David, that made CCG the perfect place to launch his consulting career, while planting the seeds for his later emergence as a civic leader. According to David, "I did a number of consulting assignments related to economic development. I saw firsthand how an independent advisory group to government could have a significant influence on public policy."

A watershed time for David in terms of shaping public policy occurred in the 1980s, when he had the opportunity to work with Neil Paget on the National Automotive Task Force. Composed of auto manufacturers and labour leaders, it had been established by Ed Lumley, Minister of Industry for Pierre Trudeau's Liberals. Its mandate was to suggest ways the government could handle the surge of Japanese small cars being imported into the Canadian market. The United States had applied voluntary restraints, and now the Liberals were being pressured to do the same. Though fleets of ships loaded with Japanese vehicles were lying off the B.C. coast, it wasn't credible for Lumley to protect the Canadian industry if the Canadian industry couldn't get its own house in order. CCG's task was to discover why the Japanese had such a major price advantage and suggest how Canadian manufacturers could improve their performance.

During this process, David met a variety of colourful characters. He especially remembered an impassioned conversation between Moe Closs, president of Chrysler Canada, and Donald Hackworth, president of General Motors of Canada. Closs was expressing concern about the impact of government-imposed pollution controls on Chrysler, as opposed to General Motors. "Don, you at General Motors are on the track in this horse race, and you have a big horse. The government says you got to carry a box of controls, and it's not a big deal because you've got that big horse. At Chrysler, I got this little horse. You put a big box on the back of my horse and I'm struggling, I'm really struggling," Closs said. "Now the government is talking about fuel economy, which is like telling me I got to run a longer race. My little horse, he finds a longer race very difficult. To your big horse, it's not a big deal. Now the gate's open, and all these Japanese horses are coming on the track. Your big horse, he'll live. My little horse, he's about to die."

In 1983, David presented CCG's 136-page report to the auto task force at the Royal York Hotel. At its core were statistics and graphs describing the high costs and poor quality that made the Canadian industry non-competitive.

Donald Hackworth of General Motors turned to Bob White, director of the Canadian United Auto Workers Union. He said, "I don't see why we're here to sell Japanese cars because I don't see anything good about them. The report's first pages about our dilemma are important. So are the last pages about how we're going to stop the Japanese. But these pages in the middle — I think we can take them out." He then picked up his Xeroxed report and ripped out about ninety pages from the middle.

Bob White said, "I think you're right. We don't need all this analysis." He ripped out the same pages, and soon everyone around the table was following suit.

David was devastated. Neil reassured him, "Don't worry, David. All those pages will be going back in. It's not credible to present a report to the government with only the few that are left."

And that's what happened, though David said he could never forget the sinking feeling in his gut at the sound of all that ripping paper.

The other thing that stuck in David's mind was Hackworth's clearly dismissive view of consultants. Setting his sights on David, the youngest and clearly most impressionable member of the team, Hackworth asked pointedly, "What did you study in college, anyway?"

David paused and answered feebly, "Philosophy."

"I thought so."

As for those Japanese carriers afloat offshore Vancouver, Lumley ordered that they be inspected to the nth degree until such a backlog occurred that the Japanese voluntarily reduced their exports. This was paired with a commitment by the Canadian industry to improve quality and lower costs in order to become competitive.

———————

In 1985, Ira Magaziner, founding partner of Telesis, based in Rhode Island with affiliates in Europe, Japan, and Australia, contacted David about a tantalizing career opportunity: Ira wanted to groom David as his business partner and right-hand man.

Ira was, as David later described him, a seductive hirer. "He had one of those pincushions where you stick phone messages, and he started pulling them out, one at a time, and reading them. 'I've been invited to a seminar in industrial policy at Harvard, but I can't go. If you were here, you'd be doing that. A senate committee wants me to testify for them, but I can't go. If you were here, you could do that for me."' Ira was telling David that he was America's go-to guy for industrial policy, and that if David joined Telesis, all the same doors would open for him.

David was flattered and excited. Telesis had some high-powered clients, like Volvo, Ford, and General Electric, to offer as enticement. He had never tested himself in global markets, and he wanted that challenge. At the same time, he wished to retain his connection with CCG and his Canadian landed immigrant status.

David left for Providence in November 1985, still driving his old Dodge Colt. For the next three years, he undertook projects in Australia, Sweden, Israel, and Mexico. He also commuted to Toronto to work on the Premier's Council.

David loved consulting, and consulting loved David. Its process — research, analysis, action — played to his talents.

He was especially interested in competitive cost analysis, developed by Telesis to a fine art. Instead of dealing in abstract theory and columns of numbers, the consulting team would figure out the cost per unit of, say, a refrigerator by counting the number of people on an assembly line and timing each process. While this might be straightforward enough if you owned the plant, the trick came in getting the same kind of information from your competitors.

In one guerrilla action, Telesis targeted the Japanese television industry on behalf of General Electric. Since GE imported many Japanese VCRs, a GE team was given permission to tour Hitachi and Toshiba Matsushita factories. As preparation, GE engineers laid out the process of television manufacturing for the team — how many parts each unit had and how they fit together. Then they assigned each member a priority task to determine how many Japanese were working on each component, how fast each machine was going, and so on. As the Americans toured, they would ask apparently random questions. By the time they had finished, they had enough information to establish the cost structure of the entire factory.

Later, when GE and Hitachi decided to jointly manufacture picture tubes, the Japanese revealed their costs. Telesis had come within 2 percent in their secondhand analysis.

In the late 1980s, Ira Magaziner and his senior partners decided to sell Telesis to the consulting firm Towers Perrin, which had also purchased the Canada Consulting Group. While David understood the Telesis senior partners' desire to cash out, he was not happy with that decision. Several years later, in 1991, he and six other partners repurchased CCG from Towers Perrin and then merged it with The Boston Consulting Group.

The first step — buying CCG — required an iron fist in his velvet glove. David was no longer the kid who delivered phonebooks from a used Dodge Colt or the novice in the green polyester suit. Now that CCG's founding partners were retiring, David was by far the company's largest revenue earner. He was able to say to the remaining partners, "If I leave instead of buying the company with you, you're not going to have much business here." As he later explained, "I wasn't trying to be threatening. I was just trying to make the facts obvious."

The deal he offered Towers Perrin for his majority stake was unusual. He would nominally pay his share of the purchase price, offset with work that he would sell back over the next two years to anyone working for Towers Perrin. As he put it, "If I sell a project and I can employ Towers Perrin people, you will give me a dollar for dollar credit against the purchase price."

David's confidence in his own ability to generate outside revenue proved so well placed that he ended up "buying" CCG for free. As he summed up, "I don't think anyone had any hard feelings over the deal, but they were surprised, very surprised." It took a year to "earn" the buy-back, and on January 1, 1993, the two firms were officially merged.

One early challenge was getting Canadian price points up as high as American price points, so that consulting would cost the same on both sides of the border. Previously, CCG had been interested in companies of $400 and $500 million. Now they had to pursue bigger ones. This strategy also affected the Canadian consulting firm's starting salaries, which automatically established payment up the line to the senior partners. Though it took a few years, David was proud that CCG established itself as a market leader in raising both billing rates and salaries so that the border evaporated and combined consulting practice became one market. As he said, "George Stalk and I used to joke that we should receive thank you notes from hundreds of Canadian grads who no longer had to choose between a high-salary consulting offer in New York and a lower one in Toronto." That reciprocity didn't happen in investment banking. For twenty years, promising candidates were faced with a big choice between New York and Toronto, providing quite different economic futures.

Out of respect for his CCG partners, David was keen on a diplomacy of language that would honour their proud heritage. The receptionist's telephone greeting began as, "This is the Canada Consulting Group of The Boston Consulting Group, how may I help?" then transitioned over time into "This is The Boston Consulting Group." As David said, "We spent a bit more on stationery, but it assured the Canadians that this was a genuine merger and not an acquisition, even though the two companies were obviously not equal in clout."

Honouring the Canadian alumni as part of the BCG alumni was another great decision. In 1995, a black-tie dinner at Toronto's Design Exchange marked CCG's twenty-fifth anniversary and BCG's thirty-fifth anniversary. As David observed, "We made a video of CCG history, and it was probably the only time the CCG founding partners had been together since the seventies. They loved it!" This also signalled to CCG's Canadian clients that BCG considered them important.

David credited George Stalk, his co-founding partner from BCG, for much of the merger's success. Theirs was a good dynamic. George let David's imagination fly while providing wisdom that acted as ballast. As David put it, "George was part of the DNA of the Boston group, and I think the two of us together were well suited to convey the passion for ideas, the passion for analytics, the passion for competitive advantage. The Canadians discovered that BCG was fundamentally an easy network to navigate, thanks to George's ability to open doors."

As a founding partner of BCG in Canada, David's career went into overdrive.

His most important client — a leading appliance manufacturer — had been acquired while he was still at CCG working on the BCG merger. The client had considered manufacturing stoves in Mexico to take advantage of lower wages, as one of their competitors was doing. But no matter how they crunched the numbers, they couldn't figure out how the competitor was able to ship from Mexico and still be so competitive. Again, it was classic benchmark analysis that solved the riddle. They were not only using trains while David's client was using trucks, but they had specially designed boxcars that would carry more stoves. They had more workers on the assembly line, they were using a simpler design for their stoves, and they had forced some of their suppliers to move to Mexico.

The client's management was astonished at CCG's ability to discover facts and figures that had eluded their own people, especially those dealing with parts procurement. As David hovered at the back of a meeting composed of some forty executives, the procurement manager asked him, "Which one is that asshole Pecaut? I hear he's saying we're doing a bad job of procurement."

David introduced himself, then persuaded the procurement manager to meet with him later. After much one-sided yelling, David suggested that the manager hire him to analyze procurement. "We didn't do a full analysis of supply. That wasn't our assignment, so why don't you have us look for opportunities to consolidate suppliers the way our competitor is doing? As manager, you should be the one leading the process."

After laughing heartily at the absurdity of hiring that "asshole" Pecaut, the manager did just that. Later, when the CEO asked for an advance briefing, David annoyed the CEO by refusing, since it was the procurement manager who had hired him. This frankness built a culture of trust between David and his client that lasted over twenty years, during which the company grew from a $1-billion company to a $15-billion one.

Another successful cost analysis focused on a money-losing plant in Indiana. This became known internally as the "complexity project" because of the way in which the Indiana management had built complexity into every aspect, from the number of products to the plethora of brands, and even the way in which the plant was laid out. By tracing every aspect of this complexity back to its cost, then simplifying each process, the company achieved a $250-million turnaround in two years.

When dealing with companies that had unions, David understood that it was necessary to get their leaders to the table and to be transparent with them.

In 1994, Canadian Airlines was suffering financially. They were competing as a smaller airline against Air Canada, which had recently privatized. They had already had one restructuring of their union agreements. How could they ask for more concessions?

With management's endorsement, the BCG team held a meeting with the six unions to explain their intention of functioning as an honest broker. "We will provide you, equally and confidentially, with all the information we give to management on their competitive and financial situation and everything else. We want you to participate in finding a solution that will save the airline without cutting your wages, if that's at all possible. We're going to look at work rules, productivity, and marketing, with wage-cutting only as a last resort."

Though the unions had to be persuaded to participate, they ended up becoming fully engaged, with machinists using stopwatches to check on the turnaround times of 747s at airports and so forth. An important part of the psychological process was the union leaders' need to vent at management over previous decisions, requiring the airline executives to practise grace under assault.

BCG determined that a 24 percent cut in labour costs was necessary to make the airline competitive. By examining the work rules in every union contract, the BCG team discovered they could save that money without cutting wages. However, the rule changes were not neutral: Where three attendants had worked a flight, now there might only be two, and a 747 pilot might fly only eleven days a month.

The BCG team had a number of brainstorming meetings in hangars across the country, presenting their plan to thousands of employees. Ironically, all the unions that BCG thought would be the most difficult signed up to the new agreement. It was the pilots' union that balked. They were the only group that preferred wage cuts to protect their work rules. They also became seduced by the idea of buying the airline themselves. This dragged out negotiations perilously close to the time when BCG had correctly predicted Canadian Airlines would run out of money.

Another option had always lurked in the background: that Air Canada might acquire Canadian Airlines. Since Jean Chrétien's Liberals could not allow the western-based airline to fail, the government could, and did, support this merger. David suspected this solution was not displeasing to Canadian Airlines' pilots' union, though it was not the one that management had desired.

Despite the loss of Canadian Airlines as a separate company, BCG's open-door process had proven effective for working with unions, and BCG used it to successfully negotiate between a major Canadian media company and one of its unions. At the heart of that settlement was the elimination of a half-hour union break, enabling the company's $400-million facility to take in outside work, preserving and increasing jobs. BCG also gained union concessions for Algoma Steel, allowing the company to attract the investment that enabled it to survive.

David believed that consulting should be gender blind. For a study on truck stop density, consultants were dispatched in their shirts and jeans to interview truckers about their habits, including how often they took washroom breaks. Some of these interviewers were women. David also assigned a formidably competent woman, Joan Dea, as project manager for a study on steel manufacturing, fully expecting her to put on a hardhat to check all aspects of production. Unfortunately, when working internationally, female consultants sometimes came up against strong cultural biases. For one Mexican factory analysis in the 1990s, David insisted on assigning two women as project leaders against the strong objections of his client, who felt his managers would not accept their findings. At the very least, the client wanted David to make the presentation. When David interviewed the women, they insisted, as he had hoped, on presenting their own work.

David was shocked at how aggressively the Mexican executives — normally overly polite to women — hammered his project leaders with questions, trying to undermine their credibility. This went on for forty minutes, with the women providing detail after detail to support their findings. For the last hour, the room fell quiet. No more questions.

Afterwards, the client congratulated David on the women's work, but he added, "You humiliated my management team."

David replied, "They humiliated themselves by going after our leaders so aggressively. The gender problem is yours. You'll have to deal with it if we're going to continue to work together."

One tricky aspect of all long-term consultant-client relationships was surviving the transition to a new CEO and leadership team. BCG managed these transitions with great diplomacy, and David kept in touch with those who quit or were fired, even at junior levels, with a friendly phone call offering references or introductions. He was astonished at how often this simple contact, sometimes at a person's darkest hour, resulted in new clients down the road.

Given David's exposure to the higher echelons, he was often offered enticing opportunities to become a CEO or a deputy minister, or to run for political office. While he enjoyed being close to power, he did not want to be on the power ladder, where you climbed your way, rung by rung, to the top. As a people person, he loved contact with every level of an organization, along with the freedom to poke his nose into hidden and offbeat places. He loved the opportunity to discover how major corporations and governments worked on the human level. He loved the international stage. He loved finding patterns and processes that worked in one set of circumstances, then applying them to others that proved only superficially different.

David was pleased and surprised to find how often the paradigms of philosophy proved valuable in dealing with real world problems. He vividly remembered interrupting a BCG team study to announce, "I think we're in the middle of a dialectic process here." He then explained Hegel's thesis-antithesis theory, i.e., that extreme circumstances and events produce their opposites, accounting for many of the seemingly inexplicable pendulum swings of history. He was so convincing that one of the team exclaimed, "You almost make me feel that philosophy stuff is useful!"

David was passionate and persuasive in his presentation of facts. But facts alone were never enough, he insisted. "So much of the time, we hear the power of a particular fact much better through a story or an example. There are many insightful things that are written on many issues, but it's capturing that story that drives people to action."

In his view, consulting at BCG meant growing your own franchise and seeding $10 million in ideas to do $1 million worth of work. He was also a great team builder. "It was never the David show," said Marc Gilbert, a BCG partner. "Everyone was part of the journey, with never a mountain too high to climb or an ocean too wide to cross."

David credited himself with two rather unusual traits for his success as a consultant. First, he understood the importance of anomaly — those facts that didn't seem to fit, but that might hold telling clues to what was right or wrong with any situation. If two manufacturers are doing well while the rest are doing poorly, what exactly is giving those winners their edge? Second, he credited himself with a high tolerance for ambiguity. In some situations, especially when dealing with government, solutions were not clear-cut. Two opposite and competing ideas might both seem right, yet only one could prevail, or else a solution that meshed important features of each must be found.

David was unabashedly tough on competitors. While large companies often liked to employ more than one consulting firm, he always wanted 100 percent of any business. When Marc was hired by David, he asked David how to deal with competitors. David replied, "Imagine that you're at a carnival and you're playing Whack-a-Mole. When a head pops up in your field, you whack him!" To David this meant investigating why BCG wasn't the client's first and only call, then putting free resources or other perks into the client's service.

It was always the work itself that motivated David, never money.

When delivering newspapers as a kid, weeks would go by during which he'd forget to collect his payments. He never spent the monthly allowance his mother gave him for clothes. He didn't realize that his first $200 investment, made at age twelve in a bowling ball company, was turning a profit until his father found the stock amidst his papers decades later.

David's lack of interest in fashion was both exasperating and endearing. No matter how successful he became, he instinctively dressed like something out of a secondhand bin, and since he was a vigorous and messy eater, his tie often sported a stain. He couldn't differentiate between navy, black, or brown, so he sometimes headed out the door wearing different coloured shoes. Blue and purple looked the same to him, and words like *magenta* could just as easily refer to some strange new life form. Before I felt I could care about his appearance, David had to care. After seeing himself on TV and videos, he began to notice: "I didn't look very good, did I?"

I would agree, "You need to dress more professionally."

David began inviting me to "meetings" in our walk-in closet to counsel him on what ties went with what shirts. Seeing that everything matched, including both shoes, became part of our morning ritual. If I was planning to be away, I taught him a few combinations that he ended up wearing day after day so he wouldn't have to experiment, because he was sure he'd get it wrong.

David hated shopping. Every couple of years we'd go to Tom's Place or Harry Rosen and have a savvy salesman pick out clothes for him to try on. He liked to buy the same things as before so he wouldn't have to learn new combinations.

One of my first gifts to David was a black briefcase to replace his Loblaws shopping bags, and he took it everywhere with him until it fell apart.

David's cars advertised, even more blatantly, his disregard for material things.

He was still driving his secondhand Dodge Colt when we began spending weekends together, and every time it rained, rivulets of rust from the car's undercarriage would run down my driveway into the gutter. Finally, someone bought it for a dollar to haul away as scrap. David's secondhand Malibu, his next car, was a big, honking gas-guzzler with a faulty exhaust that had to be driven with the windows open, so as not to suffocate the occupants. He didn't seem to notice when the muffler went as well. After we were married and I became pregnant, I picked out a pristine white Volvo station wagon as my new family car and then, in a reversal of the usual gender politics, gave him my Camry. It was in decent shape at the time, but of course he drove it to an early death.

A study by one of David's consulting colleagues demonstrated the obvious: that the price of a person's car always rose with income. Of course, David was the outlier undermining that trend.

In 1993, after a bit of research, David bought the only car he ever owned in the same decade in which it was manufactured. He chose a top-of-the-line Lexus with a great sound system, which he drove as long as his health allowed. He drove it for sixteen years, mainly to and from the office or the airport, and it was still in pretty good condition when we shipped it to our son-in-law, Matt, in California. Matt enjoyed driving that car, despite its advanced age, and listening to David's rap CD that I forgot to remove.

When buying gifts for the girls and me, David was generous to a fault. For Lauren's sixteenth birthday, he took her to buy a *used* car, and they came back with a brand-new RAV4. He did the same with Amy — this time, it was a new Volvo S40. He claimed that he had been motivated by safety concerns in buying the girls solid, reliable vehicles, but we all knew it was his generous spirit that had driven the decision.

He loved giving me extravagant gifts too. One Saturday, we pulled our younger girls in a wagon to Tiffany's, where he insisted on buying a new wedding band to replace the original that was "nice but not special."

David also loved surprises. For another birthday, I received a huge bouquet at the office with a note directing me to be outside the government building where I worked at Bay and Wellesley at five o'clock. A white limousine was parked outside, attracting a fair bit of attention. Seeing me approach with hesitation, the driver said, "Miss Burstyn? Your car." I was taken to The Room, in what was then Simpson's, where David was waiting with the manager to help me choose a few special outfits.

On another special occasion, David hired a limo to take me to Holt Renfrew, where he had arranged for what marketers would later call "an after-hours personal shopping experience." Then we were off to an intimate seven-course dinner at one of Toronto's trendiest dining spots — once again with the place all to ourselves.

David's work as a consultant routinely took him face to face with government leaders and the CEOs of multi-billion-dollar corporations. The Boston Consulting Group staged magnificent annual conferences each year for their 250 partners and spouses. Each host office would pull out all the stops to showcase their city and create an exceptional experience. In Santa Barbara, we were supplied with Hawaiian shirts, shorts, and leis for a fabulous beach party where the Beach Boys performed. In Stockholm, we took a side trip to St. Petersburg to enjoy a performance of the Kirov Ballet one night and a private tour of the Hermitage another day. In Austria and Prague, we dined and danced in castles. In Barcelona, we were treated to a circus performance. In Cannes, our hosts staged an homage to the Cannes film festival with our own red-carpet presentations for which all BCG offices produced short films to compete in one of two categories. Everything was always done in the spirit of the country we were visiting — the food, the costumes, the entertainment — and each year seemed more inventive than the year before. We were always comparing one with another, often concluding, "This one is the best!"

CHAPTER SEVEN

You Will Meet a Tall, Blond Stranger

I n 1995, David received a phone call that would be pivotal in defining the person he wanted to be and the civil society he wanted to live in. It was from United Way CEO Anne Golden, who was on a leave of absence to chair the GTA Task Force. She wanted David's help in analyzing the economy of the Greater Toronto region — an important part of the Task Force mandate when it was established by Ontario NDP Premier Bob Rae.

David, who, as usual, had too many things on the go, hedged.

Anne grew more persuasive. "This is your chance to do something huge for Toronto. I've been told that you and Boston Consulting are the right ones to do it."

David was not about to take on any more projects. "I'm sorry, but I don't have time for this."

Anne persisted, "We really should meet. I'm a tall, leggy blonde with high cheekbones."

That evening David reported to me, "I got this outrageous call from an Anne Golden who tried to persuade me to have lunch to talk about a project for the Ontario government. She claims she's a gorgeous blonde with legs that go all the way up to her neck."

I laughed out loud. "She's a short Jewish grandmother with no neck and a delightful sense of humour."

Whatever the alchemy of that original phone call, David agreed to see Anne. They met at Acqua in what was then BCE Place, the office tower where BCG was located. I had cued him to look for a short, dark-haired woman in her fifties.

Anne re-launched her pitch.

David cut her off. "Look, BCG and I are too expensive for you. You can't afford us." Before she could protest, he added, "So I'll do it for free."

Startled, Anne asked, "Why would you do for free what you wouldn't do for a fee?"

David explained, "BCG strongly supports pro bono work, and I personally think what you're doing is pretty exciting." He also wanted to send a clear signal that he was not lobbying for a consulting contract. "I need the freedom to tell it like it is as an independent third party."

This was an offer Anne couldn't refuse. When she started talking about reports and communications, David hedged again. "We don't do that. We do strategy and analysis. The person you need to talk to is my wife. She has her own consulting firm. This isn't nepotism. She's really the best person for the job."

Anne called me immediately. Since I knew the arrangement with BCG, I felt it necessary to explain that my firm was small, my rates were reasonable, and I couldn't afford to do a big job like this pro bono.

She agreed. I was hired to direct all the communications and to write, design, and deliver what Anne insisted be a first-rate report in both English and French.

Greater Toronto: Report of the GTA Task Force was published in January 1996, with David and BCG providing a very important fact-rich analysis of the region's economic strengths and weaknesses, along with a growth strategy. It showed how intertwined the 416 (the city of Toronto) and 905 (Toronto's satellite communities) were, both socially and economically, and suggested a master plan for city and suburbs to grow together, inevitably leading to amalgamation. As Anne later said, "David was indefatigable. He understood that we were in a new global era in which connectivity and innovation were critical." Then she added with her trademark humour, "And with David, don't forget the adorable factor!"

Underlying the GTA task force report was an awareness that the 1980s boom that David had found so invigorating on his arrival in Toronto had given way to a 1990s recession that was dragging down the whole country. Even as the economy improved, unemployment remained stubbornly high for those just graduating from colleges and universities. A whole generation was being stopped in its tracks by employment cutbacks, particularly in entry-level jobs. When Prime Minister Jean Chrétien mused publicly about levying a training tax on companies to help unemployed youth, employers protested that this would put an even bigger chill on the job market.

This dialogue attracted David's interest. The Premier's Council had sharpened his awareness that convening groups of key people could be a powerful tool for social change and that education had to be central to building a more prosperous, sustainable economy. With characteristic boldness, and with the help of Michael McAdoo, former executive assistant to Chrétien and now a BCG consultant, David approached the prime minister's office with a personal offer to tackle the problem on a pro bono basis. Chrétien readily agreed.

With the support of a BCG team headed by Lucille Joseph, David assembled a group of about twenty-five company executives to brainstorm. They concluded that the smartest solution for youth unemployment would be an internship program that would give young graduates that all-important first job opportunity. For relatively low compensation, they could acquire business experience in their fields and demonstrate their talents to a prospective employer.

The result was Career Edge, a national youth internship program announced in 1996 with a widely circulated photo of Chrétien and David shaking hands. Instead of asking the federal government for money, the Career Edge board asked them to join other employers in contributing intern placements in different departments across the country. The program was so successful that within a couple of years the start-up money advanced by the initiating companies had been repaid and Career Edge had become self-funding through fees paid by employers. To date, over ten thousand interns have been placed with some one thousand employers, providing meaningful entry-level experience for up to twelve months. Though participants were not guaranteed jobs, more than 90 percent did find full-time employment.

Through his pro bono contribution to Career Edge and to the GTA Task Force, David had unknowingly laid the foundation for his most satisfying life's work as a civic entrepreneur with Toronto as his platform. It would take another six years for this vision to crystallize.

————————

Given all the changes David and I had undergone since the birth of two more daughters, inevitably we had issues. Though David and I were compatible and complementary in so many ways, we were also the Odd Couple. I was the neat one and he the messy one. I was always on time or early, he was always late. He was also a pack rat who insisted on keeping every issue of *The New Yorker* for a year, even then growing anxious as I pitched each one out. He complained that if he didn't read a newspaper the moment it arrived, he would have to forage for it in the recycling bin. But David also liked my managerial side. He liked the fact that I had a career and had been doing just fine as a single mother before he came along. He liked that our fridge was always filled, our meals were always beautifully prepared and presented, and our social calendar always full of interesting people and activities. I used to joke that David believed in magic because all these things happened without his ever having to do more than wish for them.

We had interesting and often provocative conversations about books, politics, investments, anything. David could take a thought anywhere, and he was always pushing boundaries, mostly in a good way. He could easily come up with ten ideas in a half-hour, to which my response would be, "Let's pick a couple of the best ones and work with those." David wanted to write an inspirational magnum opus, and I would say, "Let's start with a chapter, something bite-sized I can help you shape."

I like rooms to be well designed, warm, and inviting, while David cared only that furniture be comfortable enough to sit on. And the man who pursued innovation in all other aspects of his life liked his home environment to remain unchanged. At one point, I completely redecorated the living room — new wall colour, new furniture, new window coverings, new everything. Amy, who loved design and was well aware of David's shortcomings in this area, predicted it would take weeks for him to notice. She was right. For nearly two months, between trips to Australia and other parts of the world, he would go into the living room, play the piano, come out again, go back in and read. Oblivious. No comment. One day, he finally asked, "Did you move something in the living room?"

While David lacked any interest in material things, he was remarkably attentive to the most important thing in his life: his family. He was a devoted father, full of curiosity and joy, bursting with enthusiasm for the girls' every new achievement or utterance. He couldn't have been more proud! For Amy's sixth birthday, we staged a teddy bear picnic, with David dressed as a giant teddy bear in my old raccoon coat, earmuffs, fluffy mittens, and slippers. For Becca's third, I rented a Barney costume for him. It was a stifling hot day in September, and the fan inside its headpiece broke. Poor David, dripping in sweat, managed to dance and sing along with the Backyard Gang, composed of Amy and friends, and entertained a dozen preschoolers, all tugging at his tail. There was nothing that guy wouldn't do to make his daughters happy. They actually thought he *was* Barney!

We were a celebrating family. We always honoured both Christmas and Chanukah (which we called Christmakah), as well as Passover and Easter.

For Christmas, we had an oversized tree with ornaments — some from David's childhood, some from our family vacations, so that each glowed with memories. No matter how old the children became, we always read the same four books: *Peef the Christmas Bear*, *The Night Before Christmas*, *Eloise at Christmastime*, and *How the Grinch Stole Christmas*. Some of our gifts were extravagant, some simple, but all were thoughtful.

Finding the perfect Christmas tree was an annual ritual that David and our younger girls, particularly Becca, relished. The mission was the same every year: bring back a beautiful, bushy tree, no more than nine feet tall, preferably a balsam with sturdy needles to support all those ornaments. Inevitably, David chose a tree that was too tall and that had to be taken down after we'd managed to raise it so he could saw off its base. Wrestling that unwieldy tree upright once again, then stringing the lights, took the better part of a day. Sighing, the kids would wander off, leaving us to squabble and struggle. "Call us when it's time to decorate."

For Passover, my family traditionally celebrated at my uncle and aunt's. After David and I began dating, but before he'd met my extended family, I asked them if I could bring him to the Seder. Since he wasn't Jewish, Uncle George thought it would be better not to include him yet. When I said I wouldn't be coming either, my aunt called me back, defying her husband probably for the first time ever: "You come and you bring your boy, too!"

The irony is that no one came to love David more than Uncle George, and no one came to love Passover more than David. He participated with great gusto, and everyone was impressed by how much he ate — second helpings, thirds! — and how closely he followed the Haggadah, in both Hebrew and English.

Our family was just as enthusiastic about Easter. The night before, we would decorate three dozen eggs that I, as the designated Easter bunny, would get up early to hide — ground floor only! I added just as many chocolate eggs, being careful to keep the dog away so she wouldn't sniff them out and eat them. Then the girls would run around with their baskets to see who could find the most. After the hunt, we enjoyed our Easter brunch (always eggs Benedict, a Pecaut family tradition) in the dining room, where we ate every meal, both as a family and with guests. It was the heart of our home.

Though David's family was very involved with their Episcopal church, they embraced the fact that I was Jewish. When Dottie couldn't find copies of her favourite New Zealand book of prayer in Sioux City, I bought them for her at Toronto's Anglican bookstore on Bloor Street. Several months after David and I married, we travelled to Mauritania, in West Africa, for the wedding of David's youngest sister, Shelley, to Youssouf Abdel-Jelil.

Though Shelley had lived in Mauritania during her time with the Peace Corps, she and Youssouf met through mutual friends in Washington, D.C. Youssouf's father, a respected, learned man of the scholarly poet caste, had passed away when Youssouf was seven years old. Youssouf was working in the Ministry of Planning as the head of the Economic Cooperation Division in Mauritania's capital, Nouakchott, where the wedding would be held. Youssouf's worldliness and Western sensibilities were surprising for someone whose recent ancestors had been nomads and whose brother lived in the desert, where the tradition of men having multiple wives was still common.

The families met at a pre-wedding party hosted by the groom's family. The women in the Sioux City contingent wore mulafahs (colourful ankle-length cotton robes) while the men sported boubous (long shirt-like garments worn over pants). Since Mauritania was a "dry" country because of its alcohol restrictions as well as its climate, we brought our hosts a goat, as was the custom, instead of a bottle of wine. We named him Freddy — a mistake, given his inevitable fate at the dinner table. The wedding party spoke a variety of languages: the local Arabic dialect, English, and French. While we were sitting cross-legged, eating with the fingers of our right hand as custom decreed, Youssouf's mother asked Dottie, with Shelley translating, whether she and her husband were from the same tribe. Dottie replied thoughtfully, "No, I'm from the Chicago tribe and my husband is from the Sioux City tribe."

Youssouf's mother replied just as thoughtfully, "It's sometimes very difficult when you're from different tribes."

We all nodded sagely.

Shelley and Youssouf's wedding was probably the biggest the region had ever seen: a five-tent, fifteen-goat affair with some two hundred guests. The goats were supposed to be provided by the bride's father. Since Dick was less than enthusiastic about selecting them, David volunteered for that honour. I went with him and Youssouf to the market in Nouakchott, an open-air dirt yard thick with dried goat pellets that slid underfoot like ball bearings.

Youssouf and the manager of this small stockyard instructed David, "To test the goat for meatiness, you feel the inner thigh of its back leg."

Trying to look nonchalant and experienced, David slid his hand between the legs of the first goat, then squeezed. The goat shot up into the air with a terrible screech. David had grabbed a testicle! Though he tried to pretend that's what he'd intended, he dissolved with laughter like the rest of us.

Youssouf told him, "Now you'll have to buy that goat."

Suddenly, all the other sellers were holding up their goats, "Squeeze mine! Squeeze mine!"

David loved telling that story, but every time he did, he increased the number of goats for the wedding. Last I heard, it was twenty-four.

Youssouf's young nephew Abdel Jelil attached himself to David, wanting to show him all the sights. Though Abdel Jelil and I could converse in French, David's version was fractured at best. I used to joke that he'd mastered English so completely he had no room for another language. While the three of us were eating together, Abdel Jelil told us an amusing story. David tried to reply in French, "You make me laugh!" Suddenly, Adel Jelil jumped up and ran into the kitchen. David was perplexed. "Did I offend him?'

I explained, "You told him to make you some rice."

That became one of our inside jokes. When we made each other laugh, we would say, "You make me rice."

———————

In August of 1996, David received some devastating news. Dottie had once again been diagnosed with cancer — not the kind from which she had recovered, but another that was rare and incurable. It was heartbreaking to see this woman of such energy and compassion wither away. Though she never entirely lost the sparkle in her bright blue eyes, they did grow dimmer. Her deep spiritual beliefs kept her calm, centred, and accepting. She declined all heroic measures — no risky, radical surgeries or IVs. She wanted to remain active as long as she could, especially with her ministry as an Episcopal deacon comforting the afflicted. She never asked, "Why me?" With Dottie, it was, "Why *not* me? I've been so blessed."

One day at his mother's bedside, David asked if she had any advice for him. She told him, kindly, "You have a great gift for listening if only you would use it more. Sometimes you aren't as mindful of others as perhaps you should be, talking over them instead." Though she had been disappointed when David broke with the church, she asked only that he remain "spiritually open." She also said, "Nothing you achieve or to which you aspire will mean as much to you in the end as your family and friends."

David took that to heart. Family had always come first with him, too. And though it was his father whom he, as a young man, tried to impress, it was his mother's voice that guided him throughout his life to make the best choices.

Dottie lived ten months after her terminal diagnosis. She spent the time at home as she had wanted, allowing David's brother, Dan, to benefit from quiet time with her. Since he lived across the street, he dropped in every evening after work, so it was as if he were a ten-year-old again, telling his mother about his day, but now having her all to himself. The whole family had been trained as doers, and at first Dan worried about what to say or how to act, but Dottie always told him, "Just be" — a thought he returned to many times.

Dottie died peacefully at her home on July 9, 1997, age sixty-six. She left her immediate family and thirteen grandchildren. While she had won many honours during her life, she was too unassuming to allow anything to be named after her. On her death, a beautiful conservation area, the Dorothy Pecaut Nature Center, was dedicated to her. A haven for school outings and summer camps, the Center is a tribute to Dottie's love of nature and her passion for education.

CHAPTER EIGHT

Fast Forward

Around the millennium, everyone on Wall Street was walking around with a cellphone glued to one ear. Business was fast and fluid, especially in New York, and in the time it took to stride from one block to another the next big deal had been completed. Though most traditional companies still considered e-commerce a fledgling notion, trailblazers like Amazon and eBay were demonstrating the astonishing impact of browser technology on sales, hinting at a future without limits.

David was no geek. After BCG's first internal election using an electronic ballot, he was embarrassed to learn only two officers had voted manually. He knew he was one of them. But David was also lightning quick at catching trends. He saw the possibilities inherent in a dot-com economy. He felt it necessary for BCG to confirm itself as the industry leader by serving present clients in this unfolding universe while attracting new ones.

David volunteered to lead BCG's e-commerce charge, not as a separate practice but as one that cut across all BCG practices. In typical fashion, he set about "climbing the rock wall" the way he always did: by talking to and learning from the field's leading-edge experts. As he said, "I networked like crazy while reading everything about web technology I could get my hands on."

In 1997, executives at David's most important client had begun to consider the potential for direct sales of their appliances on the web. To help them create a strategy, David researched how consumers shopped for durable items like appliances and cars that had to be replaced only every five to ten years. Did purchasers need to metaphorically kick their tires, or would they buy online?

From years of testing, this major manufacturer knew its products outperformed others in the laboratory, but how to get this message to consumers? One of a few recognized high-quality branding tools was the Good Housekeeping Seal of Approval. Up to this point, the company had been one of BCG's regular fee-paying clients. After some soul-searching, BCG decided that exceptional times called for exceptional measures. Instead of just researching and advising, David proposed a three-way partnership between BCG, the client company, and the Hearst Corporation, owner of the Good Housekeeping Seal. David suggested to Hearst that they create a process by which all appliances would be tested every year by objective third parties, creating a standard for North American consumers. This testing could expand to include other products, such as cellphones, creating an outstanding brand both on and offline.

Hearst was pleased to regenerate the Good Housekeeping Seal by partnering on this online start-up business. It meant acquiring dot-com space, buying appliances for testing, then creating a testing institute. As David enthused, "We all had stars in our eyes. So often consulting work must be confidential, with any disclosure causing competitive difficulties for clients, but everyone was very comfortable about being part of our public story, and appliances were something familiar and concrete that's easy to talk about."

The payoff was a major story in a leading business magazine.

Though dot-com retailers were popping up everywhere, no one was tracking their sales and providing comparisons. David decided to capitalize on this lack of good electronic data. He proposed another partnership between BCG and shop.org, a nascent trade association for online retailers and the digital division of the National Retail Federation, made up of a dozen members. His BCG team would use detailed surveys to chart the online sales of both dot-coms and traditional retailers attempting to work the web, as well as track which ads and strategies were effective. Their payoff would be an extremely useful sales database, with shop.org providing third-party credibility.

As David made clear, "Media savvy was built into our operation from the beginning. Since the media was going to help us ride the dot-com tsunami, we had to develop information that would fit their deadlines and fill column inches in a mutually beneficial way."

When it came to media mentions, David strove to get the number one e-commerce ranking for BCG. David was proud of the fact that shop.org's Christmas sales statistics appeared on the front page of the December 27, 1998, *Wall Street Journal.* This publicity resulted in a virtuous circle in which one favourable result gave rise to another. Clients with whom BCG had never worked, such as Estée Lauder and Barnes & Noble, began coming to them for e-commerce advice in climbing their own rock walls.

David's work with Len and Steve Riggio, two brothers who ran Barnes & Noble, provided him with one of his most dramatic e-commerce experiences. As owners of the company that dominated traditional book retailing, the Riggios were not in the habit of engaging consultants — not until the spectacular rise of Amazon forced a response. Here was a flourishing incumbent, without many competitors, dealing with perhaps the most successful online business ever.

At the core of the B & N dilemma was their loyalty card, purchased for $25, and entitling a customer future discounts. How would that work online? Would shrinkage in the physical book trade force B & N to reinvent their entire business philosophy?

The BCG team did a classic analysis of the future of the retail book business in which they predicted there would be few pure offline and online customers. Most would purchase in both categories. Many B & N customers were already shopping at Amazon, not just because of price differentials but also because of Amazon's impressive selection.

In BCG's estimation, Amazon did not yet have enough market share to secure their ultimate victory. Barnes & Noble had an eighteen-month tipping point to completely transform their business in order to gain the upper hand. This would involve hard choices, such as changing the loyalty program that was their main profit-earner. It was high-risk either way, though the riskier option would be to challenge Amazon at its own game.

"One of the challenges consultants have with clients is persuasiveness. We had the whole BCG New York team in the room, making their last big push to convince Barnes & Noble to make the change. The Riggio brothers were terrific — really emotional Italian New York guys with a wonderful management team. BCG made a marvellous presentation, then Len Riggio gave this incredibly passionate three-minute speech about how he'd built the business: 'I'm not going to say I'm smarter than you guys. You want to run this business? You want to put everything my family has built at risk? Be my guest!' He pulled out his ring of keys and threw them onto the table. Then he walked out of the room," David said, describing the Riggio brothers' moment of decision. "I looked at his brother, the chief financial officer, and everyone else, and I said, 'I have a feeling he'll be back.' We waited two minutes. The door burst open and he came through. He said, 'Give me those keys back. This is my company. You may be right, but I'm not ready to do this.' It was a great BCG moment, and our team and the brothers remained friends afterwards. We had convinced him in his mind, but in his heart, in his gut, it was a bridge too far."

Barnes & Noble fared decently for a time while Borders, their main traditional competitor, collapsed; however, Amazon went on to greater and greater heights online. As David summed it up: "I'm sure many of our clients have thought, 'These guys are smart. Maybe I even agree with them, but I'm not sure that's where I want to go.'"

David found his greatest e-commerce success in the travel industry. Again, this was an area in which BCG had deep roots, having worked with major airlines like Delta and United. This new initiative began in conversations with Delta, United, Continental, and Northwest over the threat of Expedia, a Microsoft domain built to capitalize on travel commerce. The problem for the airlines was that Expedia had seized control of their customers when it came to price and commissions.

The four airlines first attempted to buy Expedia, already deep into plans for its initial public offering. Through a Harvard friend on the Microsoft team, David arranged a meeting in the BCG New York boardroom — an event he would later describe as a career high point in terms of the stakes, tension, excitement, and implications. His intention was to offer a price in excess of that offered by the underwriters. That was the carrot. The stick lay in convincing Microsoft that, if they refused the buyout, the airlines would create a competitor.

Microsoft turned down the offer, probably out of pressure from Expedia's founders, who promised equity under their original plan. They probably also thought the airlines were bluffing. They weren't. Delta, United, Continental, Northwest, and BCG created Orbitz as their web presence — another start-up, this time headquartered in Chicago. Orbitz persuaded virtually every international and domestic airline to sign up, as well as to pledge to make their lowest web-advertised prices available on Orbitz. Since the site was open to all airlines, Washington granted antitrust approval — sidestepping an anticipated hurdle.

For the airlines, the biggest plus was in preventing a single entity like Expedia from gaining control of ticket distribution. The net result turned out to be lower distribution costs that were passed on to the consumer. Though Orbitz attempted to organize hotels in the same way, no general agreement among them could be achieved. Instead, hotel.com seized their inventory, taking both profit and customer contact away from the hotels as the suppliers. Ultimately, it became a company worth billions.

BCG continued its successful expansion into travel space in a number of innovative ways. One was Site 59, a business entirely owned by BCG that combined deep discounts on hotels and airline tickets to produce rock-bottom packages. The site's name meant "last minute" — i.e. the fifty-ninth minute — and the company capitalized on the fact that airline prices shot upward till flight time, then plummeted to zero when the plane was on the tarmac with an empty seat. Airlines liked the fact that pricing was opaque — meaning the cost of the reduced ticket was never displayed. Customers liked the ridiculously low prices — $180 round trip from New York to Memphis to see Elvis Presley's Graceland, including two nights at the Hilton. Once launched, sales on Site 59 doubled almost every week — a classic web success story!

David was feeling restless. He was the kind of guy who liked to build from the ground up. He wanted to start his own dot-com company, with New York as its obvious base.

I wasn't sold on the idea. First, I was unwilling to uproot our family of four daughters, ages six to nineteen. Second, I still considered BCG to be a wonderful fit for David. I knew David found it difficult to be one jostling ego in a field of shooting stars, but I didn't feel his need to distinguish himself was the right motivation for radical change.

In 2000, David formed a company called iFormation, to be funded by BCG in partnership with the investment firms Goldman Sachs and General Atlantic Partners. To help launch this new venture, David again assembled a stellar team, including Candy Lee, formerly of Torstar, and ex-BCG consultants Sara Allan and Geoff Campbell.

With iFormation based in New York, David was required to commute each week.

He had always instructed our daughters, "Call me on my cellphone when you want me. Don't ever worry about where I am." It had never seemed unusual for him to receive a call asking, "Daddy, can you pick me up from school today?" to which he might reply, "Oh, I'm sorry, but I'm in Paris." Now he was explaining to colleagues and customers why his mobile number bore a Toronto area code, since he was supposed to be based in New York.

By now, it had become clear to David and everyone involved in their online business venture that appliances were extremely difficult to sell online. The site was receiving plenty of traffic, but consumers really *did* want to open refrigerator doors, check out colours not always true online, and talk to salespeople. The company was supposed to receive revenue from sales the site forwarded to retailers, but customers were using its online resources for information, then heading to the nearest appliance store.

The company was sold in 2000 for a nominal sum. Even its initial success, spearheaded by a zingy name and an ability to scoop media attention, ended up working against it. *Fortune* published a retrospective dissecting its failure and, especially painful for David, quoting his rosy promises. He was philosophical: "Part of being an entrepreneur is looking at the upside, capitalizing on your learning, and not making the same mistake twice." More importantly, he was grateful he did not lose the trust of this long-standing BCG client. The CEO told him, "It really meant a lot to me that BCG was willing to commit to an equity position and to take risk beside us. We know in business that if we bat .300 to .400 we're doing great. I don't regret for a minute that we did this."

After creating iFormation, David acquired Site 59 from BCG so that his iFormation partners, Goldman Sachs and General Atlantic, also became partners in it.

On September 11, 2001, David's plane from Toronto was one of the last to land at LaGuardia before all American airports were closed. He didn't understand what was happening until he heard the radio reports while crossing the 59th Street bridge in a taxi and then saw the World Trade Center in flames. Site 59's office was only a few blocks from Ground Zero, and some employees took transit to the station under the World Trade Center. It was a great relief when all were accounted for after a frantic day of searching.

The impact of the 9/11 disaster on Site 59 was huge, since the company was soon handing out rebates. It recovered remarkably quickly, and business again began doubling every couple of weeks. Eventually, Travelocity purchased Site 59 at a high markup, causing Larry Kellner, CEO of Continental Airlines, to tell David, "You and BCG were three for three with us. You did Orbitz, then you did Site 59, both of which were absolutely wonderful for us. You also saved us money in other ways. You guys really got it right."

While iFormation was experiencing its ups and downs, David's and my professional relationship was undergoing its own bumpy ride.

As part of its marketing and media strategy, iFormation published a series of reports, called *Shop.org*, to showcase BCG's web savvy for the National Retail Federation. My company, Advance Planning, designed and wrote many of them.

David and I had worked well together on the Premier's Council because of the excitement of the project and the blossoming of our personal relationship. Now, however, our business roles were reversed. David, as CEO of iFormation, was my client, and one of the most demanding I had ever had. He liked things to turn on a dime, and everything seemed possible to him if only the right person were doing the job right.

I also worked with David on other reports, notably *Fast Forward* for the Canadian E-Business Opportunities Roundtable that David co-chaired with John Roth, CEO of Nortel Networks. Based on the Premier's Council model, the Roundtable convened assorted leaders and government representatives with the goal of accelerating Canada's participation in the Internet economy. Recommendations included making government services available online and changing current tax and securities regulations to prevent promising Canadian start-ups from moving to the United States.

David loved to tell the story of meeting with Paul Martin, then federal Liberal finance minister, at the Royal York Hotel — actually, in a small room off the kitchen, because nothing else was available. David had invited Jesse Rasch, a jeans and T-shirt guy who had co-founded WebHosting.com, Canada's first web hosting company, serving clients in 147 countries. Every advisor Rasch consulted told him to move his business to the U.S. because our laws would make it extremely hard to be successful here, and eventually Rasch sold his company to AT&T for $60–$70 million. That story had a huge impact on Paul Martin, as David knew it would, convincing him of the need for policy reform, which the government then undertook.

Despite the excitement of the Roundtable initiatives, I had come to realize that David saw two kinds of people in any discussion group. Some were idea people, with whom he communicated as equals, others were takeaway people he designated to carry out tasks.

David radiated incredible warmth. He was easy to know and easy to love, but he went through a stage — and he admitted this himself — when he had to be the smartest person in the room. We were at many discussion tables together, and I was always much quieter. After one of these sessions where David dominated the discussion, he sensed my disapproval and asked, "Wouldn't you like to be the smartest person at the table?"

I said, "No, I'd prefer to be the wisest."

I believe I helped David to make that distinction, reinforcing Dottie's deathbed advice. It was repeated once again by BCG during a review he underwent for his appointment as senior vice president. Typically, David didn't think he needed performance feedback, though later he described it as the most useful he'd ever received. As he boiled it down,

"They told me I had a whiz kid approach to presenting, with lots of facts, great delivery, all that high-school debating heritage, but I came across as trying to impress when I didn't need to. What I should develop was more gravitas, so I was the person in the room who was listening to everything and able to synthesize it. In my need to electrify the room and have everyone go, 'Wow!' I was losing this other element. They also told me that my role in BCG would evolve into less the doer and more the coach. It was a big psychological shift for me, from having to be 'the man' to becoming someone who enables others to be successful."

As the oldest in an achieving family, David was imprinted with the idea that he must be the leader of the pack, the star, the most special person among special people. Making room for others was the hardest lesson he had to learn, within the family as well as outside of it.

The Pecaut children understood that their mother was an extraordinary woman who had set aside many opportunities to devote herself to her family. When she began to blossom on her own, Dick sometimes made light of her accomplishments. He never attended the art show that marked her graduation with a second bachelor degree in fine arts. Before her ordination as an Episcopal deacon, he joked about how handy she would be when he needed someone to administer the last rites. She was hurt by that. She didn't need a lot of praise, just some acknowledgment.

Dick's uneasiness was typical of males of his generation. Dottie once told me that, at board meetings, she often expressed an idea that went unnoticed until a man announced the same thing ten minutes later. Though this is now a feminist truism, I heard it first from Dottie.

When Dottie confided her frustration to David, he was quick to reply in indignation, "That's so unfair!" He was chastened when I told him, "But you do that to me sometimes."

David took considerable liberties when including me in his speeches to illustrate points he was making. I remember being at a dinner for about four hundred educators where David was the keynote speaker. David had been warning about the dangers of letting kids troll for information online. I snapped to attention when he suddenly began talking about what a great online shopper his wife was, and how, to his delight, I had started visiting the Victoria's Secret site to pick out swimsuits and lingerie. I was sitting with Veronica Lacey and other colleagues at a front table. Seeing my reaction, Veronica tapped the red tablecloth and whispered, "That's how red your face is. I can imagine how much trouble he's in."

By 2003, David was forced to admit that iFormation was a financial failure. Part of the problem was timing, which couldn't have been worse. From 1997 to 2000, BCG's e-commerce practice had risen from $8 million to over $200 million. Such growth was not sustainable. In retrospect, it would be seen that NASDAQ had peaked in June 2000, when David's company was founded. By 2002, the dot-com bubble had burst, and tens of thousands of jobs were shed across the industry.

David had come too late to the party.

This was reflected in David's pro bono work for the Canadian E-Business Opportunities Roundtable. At the January 2000 launch of its first report, *Fast Forward*, Nortel Networks CEO John Roth was treated like a rock star, with so many flashbulbs going off that he could have been U2's Bono. By the second report, launched at the Toronto Stock Exchange a year later, Roth was no longer CEO of Nortel, and Nortel was no longer an industry icon. Brian Tobin, minister of industry, was unpleasantly surprised at the poor turnout, though the reports were good and their facts and recommendations influenced federal policy by instilling the idea that Canada could become an e-commerce leader.

As usual, David chose to see his e-commerce and iFormation experiences as important for learning, while still stinging at his company's failure. He'd appreciated the opportunity to see how great business minds, like the Riggio brothers of Barnes & Noble or the father-son duo of Leonard and William Lauder of Estée Lauder, reacted when faced with out-of-the-box problems. He liked the entrepreneurial rush of creating start-ups instead of just advising. In hindsight, he was "pleasantly stunned" at how accurate most of his team's e-commerce projections turned out to be, and how much of the book business for travel, and other consumer experiences would move online. He felt that iFormation had added value to BCG's brand, for attracting business and recruits by establishing it was willing to go boldly where others feared to tread. He was also grateful that he and BCG remained on good terms with iFormation's partners, Goldman Sachs and General Atlantic Partners.

On the downside, David was an optimist who hated to say no, but the nature of start-ups is that you turn down a hundred proposals for every one that you accept. At the same time, many of the most exciting had to be rejected because they would have created conflicts of interest with BCG or with Goldman Sachs clients. David also realized that he had oversold iFormation's prospects to himself and to BCG, reflected in a too-high New York overhead, both in employees and in rent, as well as in the London and Hong Kong offices.

In 2003, David folded iFormation and returned to BCG as a full-time consultant. As he acknowledged, "There is nothing more humbling than sitting around a table with your partners after losing their money." Though David was mostly philosophical and quick to move on, he was hurting. The financial loss had created some hard feelings, and though his Toronto colleagues were frankly happy to have him back, there were those at BCG who were less welcoming. David recognized that this was a period of penance for the iFormation failure. It was a difficult time, but David got through it because he liked to think the best of everyone, and he also liked everyone to think the best of him.

John Clarkeson, the retired head of BCG, acknowledged the failure but couldn't help admiring David's pluck: "While the results were of course mixed, David stunned us with his uncanny ability to enlist the savviest names in the investment business in our quixotic enterprise." Though David was the natural choice to lead BCG's effort during the dot-com era, Clarkeson recognized, "We should have known that you never encourage David to do something you really didn't want done."

The three years David had spent commuting to New York had been hard on everyone in our family, though not as disruptive as moving to New York would have been. David and I kept Friday and Saturday nights for ourselves, while Sunday night around the dinner table was family time that we both treasured. We talked about everything, though we tried to keep business off the agenda. Whenever David couldn't contain himself, I borrowed a line from the mother of a friend: "Is this a marriage or a merger? I prefer marriage."

I borrowed another line from the wedding vows of our friends Matthew Mendelsohn and Kirsten Mercer, who had composed their own. When the groom promised to make his bride laugh every day, I gave David an elbow in the ribs and exclaimed, "Now that's a good promise!"

He replied, "So you like that, eh? Okay, I can do that."

When we were both under pressure, it was sometimes a hard promise to keep. David was such a wheeler-dealer, he'd argue on one of his funnier days, "That's three times today I made you laugh, so I'm off the hook for the next two days."

"Oh no, you can't bank laughter. It has to be a different laugh every day."

Our negotiations on this topic relieved a lot stress during a trying time.

CHAPTER NINE

SARS '03: The Stones Take Downsview

For David, Anne Golden's 1996 GTA Task Force had been a one-time pro bono act of goodwill in support of his chosen community. At the same time, it had spotlighted him to civic leaders as someone with a deep understanding of how Toronto functioned. The chain of events that would transform David into a passionate around-the-clock civic booster started in the spring of 2002.

Efforts were underway to organize a City Summit at the request of Mel Lastman, the first mayor of the newly amalgamated City of Toronto. The 1990s had ushered in a recession, deepened by the impact of 9/11 on tourism and the downloading of social services onto Ontario cities by Mike Harris's provincial Conservatives. Anxiety was building among civic leaders that Toronto — so dynamic in the 1980s — was now losing ground. A new urban agenda was needed to deal with the deterioration of the city's infrastructure and with the hangover of mutual distrust between downtown Toronto (the 416 area code) and its satellite communities (the 905). Mayor Lastman had been impressed by Montreal's recent City Summit and wanted his own summit that would bring together a brain trust of civic leaders to chart a plan for Toronto.

I received a call from the Board of Trade asking if David might be willing to speak at Toronto's June 2002 City Summit. David was very much in demand, but I thought he would be interested, especially if Summit co-chair John Tory asked him. John is the kind of guy who hears a suggestion and is immediately off and running. I wasn't surprised when David told me that evening, bursting with enthusiasm, "You'll never guess who came to see me today — John Tory. He asked me to be the keynote speaker for the June City Summit."

The first City Summit, entirely financed by the private sector, was held at the Rotman School of Management at the University of Toronto. Its four chairs, appointed by Mel Lastman, were in the forefront of the Toronto urban movement: John Tory, CEO of Rogers Cable; Elyse Allan, CEO of the Toronto Board of Trade; David Crombie, former Toronto mayor and CEO of the Canadian Urban Institute; and Frances Lankin, CEO of the United Way of Greater Toronto.

John introduced David's keynote speech in the most flattering of terms — "a world-renowned visionary, strategist, and practical business architect" — and David rose to the occasion.

He endeared himself to the audience by describing what he, as an American, had found so lovable and livable about Toronto — his old-style Italian barber, Danny, with his tiny two-chair shop in Yorkville; his Metro-Central Y basketball games with pickup teams that were "a cornucopia of Toronto's ethnic heritage"; his daughters' fledgling steel pan band at Rosedale Public School that had competed, and won, against established school orchestras in the Kiwanis Music Festival.

Having been well primed by his BCG team with facts and statistics, David laid out the GTA's strengths and weaknesses, comparing it both favourably and unfavourably to American cities like Boston and Washington. He talked about the vitality that eighty thousand immigrants brought to the GTA each year; about our thriving financial, food, biotech, and entertainment industries; about our skilled work force, with over 50 percent possessing college or university degrees; about our reasonable corporate taxes and our low crime rate.

From David's international experience, he knew the essentials for attracting the global companies that were the drivers of wealth in any urban economy. One of the most important was transportation. While our railway hub was mostly in good order, the commuter congestion on our highways was costing the GTA $2 billion annually in lost productivity. Pearson airport had excellent international service to 250 cities and 65 countries, but suffered from domination by one airline, resulting in cavalier service and the inflationary cost of intercity air travel. As he told the audience, "From Boston or New York to Washington it's $110 roundtrip, and you just get on a shuttle. From Toronto to New York, a roundtrip economy ticket today costs $1,300."

Because of overbooking, David had been bumped twice from Air Canada flights in the previous week, despite having paid full fare in advance. Two other passengers, bumped with him, were the head of the largest health care fund in the U.S. and the president of the largest health care manufacturing firm, on their way to a medical conference. They were appalled. Another headache awaited at Pearson International: Canada's customs and immigration service, an infuriating bottleneck when compared with airports in Europe.

David blew the crowd away.

Ratna Omidvar, president of Maytree, spoke for many when she said, "Here was this fellow who was helping us to see our city in a different light by comparing us to Seattle, to Boston, and putting on the table how many patents are produced in the city of Toronto versus Silicon Valley. One of his greatest capacities is to understand complex problems quickly and to communicate them in simple, graspable terms. He gave us a sense that we were a city in decline, but that it was possible to return to a place of civic dignity and prosperity."

Former Toronto Mayor David Crombie was similarly impressed that David had caught the essence of Toronto while delivering hard truths in a positive way. "People always respond better when you speak to their pride and not their shame."

By the conclusion of the City Summit, a framework had been established for bolstering the city's strengths, tackling its key challenges, and shaping its future. There was also a clamour for David to become more involved.

David was used to working globally, or at least nationally, on big issues. While he loved Toronto, he hadn't yet thought of the city as his personal project. However, he had galvanized himself as well as everyone else. The deeper he had delved, the more upset he had become at the stagnation threatening this incredibly vibrant city and its potential to be the best on earth. It occurred to him, belatedly, that Toronto *was* a big issue, something he could care passionately about. The City Summit had been for him the ultimate expression of his undergraduate thesis: the strength of weak ties.

David now began to articulate his philosophy around the role of a convener, someone who could put out the call and have everyone in leadership show up. One of his entrepreneurial friends declared the ultimate British convener to be Prince Philip. Who in Canada could deliver this kind of independent clout? Those with political power also had political baggage. As David mulled the problem, he began to feel that marrying pro bono work with convening might prove magical. He considered the City Summit to be a good foundation on which to build. He also began to see convening as a great role for himself and for BCG, with Toronto as a platform and its beneficiary.

This marked the beginning of David's reinvention of himself as a civic entrepreneur, a term first applied to him by University of Toronto professor David Wolfe, who, after reading Doug Henton's book *Grassroots Leaders for the New Economy*, thought it fit David to a tee. The two Davids had many conversations about what makes a civic entrepreneur and concluded it was largely about the ability to make connections between people. "It's challenging if you've got a busy life," admitted a too-busy David, "but I try to see everybody and be open to everyone."

The Toronto City Summit Alliance (TCSA) was founded in November 2002, with David as chair. Though it was established on the shoulders of the City Summit, typically David wanted to shape the organization in his own way. Its steering committee was composed of the four founders of the City Summit, plus some forty other powerful leaders representing universities, businesses, financial and ethnic communities, the medical profession, trade unions, youth, poverty activists, and various levels of government.

BCG donated office space, telephones, computers, and meeting rooms. It also supplied volunteer staff, as did a couple of accounting and law firms.

A few independent consultants were added, with funding provided by the corporate and union sectors, plus a sizable loan David made out of his own pocket (later repaid, though he never cashed the cheque).

David compared the first steering committee meeting to a barn raising in its spirit of cooperation and conviviality. It thrilled him to see people of diverse backgrounds bouncing ideas off each other — a cultural czar buttonholing a politician! A bank CEO talking to the president of a sports organization! A former premier engaged with the chairman of a Chinese geriatric home!

Working groups were created to support the steering committee on key issues, such as city infrastructure, financing, education, and immigration, with these broken down into subgroups like housing and the waterfront. The alliance was a "roll-up-your-sleeves" action group, focused on social and economic issues relevant to the whole GTA and pledged to go it alone if government funding was not available.

In the early days, there were a handful of people who played key roles in getting this fledgling organization off the ground. Jill Black and then Jonathan Guss were the first executive directors. Courtney Pratt, John Evans, and Liz Mulholland were also there from the very beginning, serving as the first directors of the organization when it was incorporated. "We were joined, over the years, by a remarkable array of colleagues, volunteers, and champions of every possible stripe and persuasion," recalls Liz Mulholland. "In trying to bring about the best for Toronto, David set in motion a process and a way of bringing out the best in people. The pragmatists began to dream and the dreamers got practical, cynics began to believe, curmudgeons grew friendly, leaders learned to follow, followers began to lead, unlikely friendships abounded, differences shrank, trust grew, *no*s dwindled and *yes*es ruled."

Once the TCSA got rolling and hired Julia Deans as its CEO, it became an unstoppable force. David was the magnet at the centre of this force field that was redefining civil society and attracting an ever-widening circle of engaged citizens.

As Julia recalled, "The start of David's meetings was sometimes underwhelming, but then the magic would begin. He would get us thinking bigger and bolder, till before we knew it, hours would pass, and we'd be saying yes to whatever came out of his mouth. No matter what David was talking about, whether it was poverty or mentorship or immigrants, you would get the impression that it was all he ever talked about and all he ever did."

As always, David's first concern with any group was to forge a common fact base. For example, a controversy arose in the housing subgroup about whether Toronto did or did not have a housing crisis. A low-income activist insisted it did; a major builder of condos, aware of his own high vacancy rates, insisted it did not. Of course, the question was not one of availability but affordability. The group's short-term solution: housing supplements to bridge the gap until lower-cost units could be built.

The Alliance was supported by the very best research minds and an outstanding board of engaged, respected, and articulate civic leaders. But the group was having trouble pulling all the pieces together in a report. They were on draft ten, which was still in disarray, when David asked me if I would rescue it as a favour. "And, by the way, could you also find a good inexpensive typesetter and graphic designer?"

Of course the report that David insisted would require only one day took three weeks. I shortened the overly long draft by two-thirds to thirty pages, then gave it a punchy title, perhaps reflecting my own impatience — *Enough Talk: An Action Plan for the Toronto Region*. It was focused yet substantive, visionary yet specific enough to frame a plan of action.

Essentially, the report combined the facts outlined in David's City Summit speech with the recommendations of TCSA's working groups. It addressed issues of business and finance, education, culture, poverty, housing, transportation, infrastructure, the waterfront, immigration, tourism, and research and development.

Enough Talk called for a new fiscal deal for all Canadian cities while pulling no punches when speaking locally. The GTA, with its 5 million people, was the country's driver of wealth and growth. In 2000, our financial services were the third largest in North America after New York and San Francisco; our automotive industry was the second largest after Detroit; our food and beverage manufacturing was second largest after Chicago; our biomedical and biotechnology centres were fourth largest; our business and professional services were comparable to New York, Chicago, and Washington; our film and TV production was the third largest in North America, while our English-language theatre was third largest in the world. Our aerospace industry was the world's fifth largest.

But the future of the GTA had been seriously undermined by recession and unfair pressures exerted by other levels of government. In 2000, the GTA gave the Ontario government $3 billion more than it received back. It gave the Canadian government $17 billion more than it received back. Thanks to downloading, the cost of health and social assistance in the GTA had risen from 18 percent of operation expenses in 1988 to 33 percent. Though it was popularly believed Canadian governments subsidized their cities more than our entrepreneurial American neighbours, this was a myth. Fifty percent of the GTA's revenue came from property taxes; in American cities, it was about 20 percent. While the Toronto Transit Commission had the second highest ridership in North America, it had the lowest subsidy per rider, with passengers paying 80 percent of its costs. Gridlock, costing the GTA $2 billion annually in lost productivity, was the greatest concern of local business owners and the most serious barrier to attracting new industry.

For all these reasons, the GTA as Canada's "golden goose" was suffering more than most people in and out of government realized. Something had to be done to resuscitate it. The report's recommendations included relieving cities of the provincial and federal sales and services taxes; uploading some costs back to the province; sharing gasoline-tax revenue to support urban transportation, and allowing Ontario municipalities taxing powers. The TCSA also built in roles for itself, such as reversing the decline in tourism, working strategically to develop the GTA as a world research centre, developing a plan for income security reform, and enhancing the role of arts and culture.

Enough Talk was launched at a press conference in April at University of Toronto's Munk Centre, then circulated to various stakeholders and potential partners, including all levels of government. On June 5, 2003, it was enthusiastically endorsed at the second City Summit — a "big tent" event attended by several hundred at the Metro Toronto Convention Centre.

David was delighted with the buzz that the report and the Summit created. Dalton McGuinty, then Ontario Liberal opposition leader, not only spoke at the event, but he also incorporated *Enough Talk*'s recommendations into his platform. Ontario's New Democrat Party leader, Howard Hampton, participated from the audience, as did a number of GTA mayoral candidates. Jim Flaherty, then provincial Conservative finance minister, expressed his enthusiasm. Over thirty sponsors, including some trade unions, supported the Summit with donations and endorsements. *Enough Talk* also received extensive media attention, along with favourable editorial comment, from all the major papers.

What surprised David, on coming down from this high, was the ho-hum reaction of both Ottawa and Queen's Park: *Okay, so this is what 450 people from Toronto want, but what does Toronto want?*

The TCSA drafted a letter endorsing *Enough Talk*, addressed to Prime Minister Chrétien and Premier Ernie Eves, then circulated it to the heads of major corporations, non-profit groups, trade unions, universities and colleges, requesting them to duplicate or modify it using their own letterheads. David and his team collected in excess of two hundred responses, many with personal notes to the prime minister and premier.

These had enormous impact on both Ottawa and Queen's Park, as David later learned. *Enough Talk*'s basic message — that it *did* represent the GTA in demanding a new fiscal deal for cities — made it through to both governments. Yet, as fate decreed, it was a global crisis afflicting Toronto that would prove City Summit was, indeed, more than just talk: the SARS epidemic of 2003.

An early spring outbreak of the disease had turned Toronto into a virtual no-fly zone. The World Health Organization had issued a travel advisory warning travellers not to come here. The international media was flooded with photos of Torontonians lined up for blocks awaiting needles, or wearing face masks, with hospital staff garbed head to toe in what looked like space gear. The tourism industry, employing thirty thousand people, was undergoing a $500-million to $1-billion loss. Occupancy at some motels and hotels had fallen to 10 percent. Conventions were being cancelled and thousands of employees laid off.

The federal government earmarked $10 million to rescue Toronto's tourist industry, creating a new dilemma: What organization would be able to administer the money? Tourism Toronto was used to handling only a small budget supplied by the city, and its members were the ones suffering the most. It lacked the infrastructure to frame, support, and implement an effective plan.

This was when the TCSA transformed itself from what David Crombie described as a think-tank into a "do-tank."

The TCSA partnered with Tourism Toronto, the GTA, Queen's Park, and Ottawa to design a recovery plan steered by David. In a series of phone calls, he persuaded every major Toronto bank president, along with Galen Weston and Sears Canada, to contribute the dollars needed to provide an additional $1.3 million in funding for the effort.

The idea of a benefit concert was floated by Dennis Mills, a businessman and former MP, and co-promoted with Senator Jerry Grafstein. Mills subsequently persuaded Mick Jagger and the Rolling Stones to perform at Downsview Park in north Toronto, with Molson Canadian as their underwriting sponsor. The concert was scheduled for July 30, two months after the World Health Organization removed Toronto from its SARS danger list. Overnight, Mick Jagger and the other Stones began appearing in TV ads, assuring Americans that Toronto was now safe — no face masks, no antiviral needles!

The all-day rock fest — Toront03's signature event — was a noisy, showy, fabulous triumph, hosted by actor Dan Aykroyd and featuring AC/DC, The Guess Who, Justin Timberlake, Rush, Blue Rodeo, and a dozen other performers. The Rolling Stones closed with a ninety-minute set. The benefit attracted between 450,000 and 500,000 fans, making it the largest outdoor ticketed event in Canadian history, and one of the largest in North America. As an endorsement of the Canadian beef industry, also in the doldrums because of a few recent cases of mad-cow disease, Alberta beef was featured.

The next question: How to build on this smash hit to sell the rest of the summer in Toronto? Even before SARS, the city had been doing a lacklustre job of marketing itself. Americans still saw us as the home of Mounties, maple syrup, and moose. Many of our featured attractions — the CN Tower, the Metro Zoo, the Science Centre — were decades old, and despite the vigour of our arts scene, its producers weren't cooperating to promote it.

The solution: bargains! Toront03 worked with Tourism Toronto on an aggressive marketing campaign that began by bundling hotel accommodations with a choice of entertainments, including tickets to the theatre, a Blue Jays game, and the ballet. A website and TV ads promised "Kids Go Free!" — to Wonderland, the Science Centre, the Royal Ontario Museum. Celebrities like the Barenaked Ladies and Jason Priestley created free TV promotions targeting bordering cities such as Detroit and Buffalo. Conan O'Brien brought his popular TV show, *Late Night with Conan O'Brien*, to Toronto for a week in what *Variety Magazine* called "the product placement deal of the year," since Toronto was showcased every night.

As planned, Toront03 terminated itself at the end of the year, bequeathing leftover funds and enduring assets, such as its website, to Tourism Toronto. Its meteoric rise had resulted in $70 million in incremental economic benefits for Ontario, plus a bounce-back in tourism that brought the GTA's 2004 revenues somewhat higher than the pre-SARS level. The TCSA had established its credibility by responding quickly and innovatively, by its ability to stand the test of public scrutiny in tendering contracts, and by providing value for public investments.

All this was accomplished with pro bono leadership and in the spirit of civic pride.

CHAPTER TEN

Hiring Mr. Softee

Y̲ou might remember this television commercial. A kid with attitude, dressed in a fast food uniform, is asking a new employee, "Do you know how to work a Softee machine?"

What gives the ad its bite is the new employee seeking guidance: he's a forty-something engineer from Tehran.

By 2001, Toronto had become the highest per capita immigrant city in North America. Toronto's foreign-born population was 47 percent, and the GTA's was 43.7 percent. By contrast, New York's was 24 percent; Los Angeles's, 30.9 percent; Miami's, 40.2 percent. Compounding the problem of integration was the fact that Ontario received 53.2 percent of immigrants to Canada, but only 38 percent of federal immigration funding. Meanwhile, Quebec received 15 percent of immigrants, but a whopping 33 percent of federal funding.

Most government money was focused on initial needs, such as food and housing. When it came to finding work in a chosen field, the majority of immigrants had to fend for themselves. Yet more than 60 percent of GTA immigrants had been specifically chosen for their skills, and more than half had some form of post-secondary education.

The Conference Board of Canada estimated the loss of wages due to immigrant underemployment at $4 billion a year, most of it in the GTA.

The ad's sponsor was the Toronto Region Immigrant Employment Council, founded by Maytree and the Toronto City Summit Alliance, in September of 2003, to bridge the gap between skilled immigrants and potential employers. David had circulated *Enough Talk* — the TCSA's calling card — among business leaders, one of whom was Dominic D'Alessandro, then CEO of Manulife Financial. Since D'Alessandro's family had emigrated from Italy when he was a child, working with TRIEC appealed to him. He and one of his top executives, Diane Bean, became co-chairs, supported by a steering committee that included David and Ratna Omidvar, who also agreed to be TRIEC's executive director.

As with so many problems, David found a lack of information at the core of immigrant underemployment. The previous decade had brought an influx from the Philippines, India, Bangladesh, and Pakistan — countries whose educational credentials were not familiar to Canadian employers. Though these immigrants' degrees might be as good as, say, those of a Queen's University grad, they were being refused interviews by major employers. All their contacts were within their own communities — South Asians helping South Asians, Portuguese helping Portuguese. Not only did these ethnic communities lack outside connections, but the few government agencies advising them were also not well plugged into potential employers. A third barrier was the fact that some professional regulating bodies restricted growth in part to maintain standards, but also to keep their members' incomes high.

Ratna and David met with the heads of some forty regulatory bodies to assure them that TRIEC respected their fiduciary responsibility to protect the integrity of their professions, while questioning why so many immigrants, with solid work and educational credentials, were locked out. Again, much of the problem proved to be a breakdown in information. A close analysis of immigrant nursing scores showed many failures were due to cultural differences and to unfamiliar methodology. A four-week course to teach Canadian procedures was enough to double the pass rate.

Another roadblock was the inability of immigrants to market themselves. TRIEC established a program in which business mentors pledged to spend perhaps six hours a month helping immigrants to write resumés, prep them for interviews, and then debrief them.

David mentored one man, Tim Simba, who'd been the chief marketer for the largest supermarket chain in Zimbabwe. Though David thought him to be an extremely capable fellow, Tim never received an interview call back. After asking Tim's permission to phone his last interviewer, David discovered the problem to be a one-year gap in his resumé during which he'd fled to Uganda because of violence under President Robert Mugabe. When questioned about this gap, he would grow vague and defensive, creating an air of discomfort in his interview. David explained to him that Canadians would understand these kinds of political problems if only he were honest and explicit. Sure enough, the man was successful in leaping over this hurdle to find appropriate employment.

On another occasion, a BCG woman in her early twenties, whom David had encouraged to become a mentor, consulted him over a problem similar to the one in the aforementioned ad. How was she supposed to advise a South Asian who was her father's age? His resumé was a mess, and they could barely communicate. David reminded her of her own skills: She was a university graduate, she knew how to write a resumé, and she understood his marketing background. With confidence restored, she became more patient. Ironically, the East Indian man found work at several times his mentor's own salary, for which he gratefully called her "his little angel." She was thrilled to have had such a big impact on someone else's life.

To date, the Mentoring Partnership has fostered close to seven thousand relationships between skilled immigrants and Canadian professionals. An estimated 85 percent were hired in their own occupations, with an average salary boost from $35,000 to $65,000. Fifty organizations now offer the Mentoring Partnership to their staff as an opportunity to enhance their coaching and leadership skills. TD Bank Financial Group was so impressed by the program's ability to find untapped employee potential that it introduced mentoring to other cities. This model has also been copied in New Zealand.

"Part of David's genius was in putting an operational framework around ideas other people had been working on, but couldn't get done," says Alan Broadbent, chair of Maytree. "We had been trying to integrate skilled immigrants into the work force but couldn't sell it to the business community. Then along came David."

Riding on this success, TRIEC launched Career Bridge — an internship program for young immigrants, modelled on the Career Edge program for post-secondary graduates, previously founded by David with BCG's support. For six to twelve months, its participants, over 53 percent of whom have master's degrees or higher, are placed in mid-level positions and provided with a coach. Career Bridge has provided thousands of internships, with an estimated 80 percent of its interns finding full-time employment.

Only two months after the launch of TRIEC, the TCSA tackled that most intractable of urban problems: poverty.

Over several decades, poverty in the GTA had become not only more severe but more concentrated, so that if you were poor, likely everyone on your street was poor. While poverty had declined in Canada, it had increased in Toronto, partly due to the downloading of social costs on municipalities. Some 286,000 GTA households were paying more than 30 percent of their income on housing, established as the maximum for low-income families. About 91,000 GTA households were on the waiting list for social housing. Those on social assistance — some 80,000 households — were receiving $544 to cover rent, whereas Toronto's average market-rent was $1,055. In the city of Toronto alone, some 30,000 individuals used homeless shelters annually.

In November 2003, the Alliance launched the Affordable Housing Coalition. It was co-chaired by former Toronto mayor David Crombie and Ed Sorbara of the Sorbara Group, with a steering committee that included other private-sector developers, rental-housing owners, major financial institutions, and social agencies. Its aim was to work with all three levels of government to make affordable housing a priority in the Toronto region.

A public campaign, Make Housing Happen, was launched in February 2004, with posters placed on bus shelters and recycling bins across Toronto. These directed people to a website that provided information about housing needs and how to advocate change. This fanfare helped persuade the McGuinty government to provide rent supplements, allowing people to move into available higher-priced housing.

David's awareness of United Way's "poverty by postal code" also led to creation of the Strong Neighbourhoods Task Force, co-chaired by Robert Harding, chairman of Brascan Corporation, City of Toronto Commissioner Eric Gam, City Manager Shirley Hoy, and Frances Lankin, CEO of the United Way of Greater Toronto, with the United Way also providing staff support.

The United Way study had shown that, during the 1990s, Toronto's twelve poorest neighbourhoods had a 16 percent decline in income, while the twelve richest had a 10 percent increase. This income loss was aggravated by a dramatic 43 percent decline in the use of GTA schools as community centres because of the introduction of user fees. For example, the East Scarborough Boys and Girls Club cancelled eight free after-school programs, offering floor hockey, soccer, volleyball, crafts, and board games for more than three hundred children ages six to seventeen, because user fees from 1999 to 2001 would have cost them $96,000. Since cancellations had the greatest impact on the poorest neighbourhoods, David was not alone in declaring war on this curtailment of community resources.

David's BCG team, working with the task force's co-chairs, typically began with a grassroots comparison of life in various poor neighbourhoods versus life in more affluent neighbourhoods. What was the average walking distance to the subway? How far was the nearest public library? What support was provided for women with newborns and for immigrants? Using various measurements, they found that thirteen neighbourhoods kept popping up with intense levels of poverty and disproportionate needs because they were under-resourced in terms of funds and infrastructure. These became the group's focus, with other priority areas added later.

While the United Way raised private money for community infrastructure, David and the co-chairs pursued the same kind of tripartite agreement with three levels of government that had already been achieved in Winnipeg and Vancouver to help their impoverished neighbourhoods. Between 1995 and 2000, Winnipeg had received $75 million, and was due for a fourth agreement in 2003. The Toronto team was on the verge of success when Paul Martin's Liberals fell to Stephen

Harper's Conservatives. As a result, they received only partial funding, not the full amount they had targeted. Nevertheless, the United Way and Toronto continued their efforts to bring resources to those thirteen communities, while the province established a program to underwrite user fees so that schools could once again serve as community hubs.

In addition to his work with the TCSA, David joined the national board of Pathways to Education, a program created by the Community Health Agency in Regent Park. Its goal: to keep kids productively in school and boost high school completion rates.

In Grade 9, participating families would sign a Pathways contract that provided each kid with after-school tutoring, a $1,000 college or apprenticeship scholarship for every completed high school year, and mentoring that emphasized career possibilities previously considered beyond reach. An advocate was assigned for every forty kids to track down those who skipped school and to provide counselling and relevant support services to those dealing with abuse and other issues. Since the advocate provided transit fare every two weeks, the kids had an incentive to go to school and keep in touch.

Pathways lowered the high school dropout rate in Regent Park from 56 percent to 12 percent, while raising university attendance from 20 percent to 80 percent, with only 5 percent attrition — far below the national average.

As a spur to Pathways' expansion, BCG did a pro bono cost-benefit analysis of the program, based on hard, quantifiable factors, such as higher incomes producing higher tax revenue. For every $1 invested, they found a $24 return, with a per student cumulative lifetime benefit of $600,000. David was also impressed by a 25 percent drop in Regent Park's crime rate at the same time rates had risen in adjacent neighbourhoods. This decrease had followed Regent Park's "summer of the gun": an unprecedented eight youth-on-youth murders. Teenage pregnancy had simultaneously fallen by 75 percent.

The Ontario Trillium Foundation, the provincial government agency that I chaired, had been the first funder of Pathways through a grant that later allowed the program to be adapted in other communities with high dropout rates. Major funding from government had been a harder sell because, at $4,000 per youth, it was considered a costly program. The BCG analysis helped convince the province to spend $20 million to grow the program, with the Pathways' board raising another $20 million from private sources. The program has since been rolled out to Rexdale, Lawrence Heights, Scarborough, Ottawa, Kitchener, Hamilton, Kingston, Montreal, Halifax, and Winnipeg, with equally good, or even better, results.

David credited much of Pathways' initial success to the street legitimacy of Regent Park's Community Health Centre, where it began. As he had learned in his undergrad research in East Boston, you couldn't just drop a project into a community. You needed an anchor — a trusted and familiar hub, such as a health centre, a Boys and Girls Club, a school organization — to legitimize it through the strength of weak ties.

You also needed to demonstrate social return on investment — something governments and other funders were increasingly wrestling with in trying to decide which worthy projects to support. BCG's pro bono analysis of Pathways' success in reducing crime and creating employment was compelling, and the case for funding became clear.

"David was a big part of what made Pathways successful," said Sam Duboc, Pathways' chair. "David had this innate curiosity, and an unbelievable ability to get things done."

For David and many other civic leaders, Pathways to Education became the model for turning a thriving community initiative into a national success story.

CHAPTER ELEVEN

A Cuisinart with No Off Switch

D avid's first illness crept up on him by stealth. Though he'd had minor symptoms, it wasn't until he showed me a toilet full of blood that we knew something was terribly wrong.

This was in early June 2004. We had to wait three weeks for the pathology report, while doing our best to pretend everything was normal. It wasn't. David had colon cancer.

That was a hard message to absorb, especially since David was still playing pickup basketball twice a week and enjoying long cross-city jogs. After one such run, he described to me blowing past a younger fellow as they raced up a hill, and thinking, "I'm in this great shape, and yet I have cancer?"

I was more fatalistic. When I heard that diagnosis I feared the worst, but I never admitted it, because in David's world nothing bad was allowed to happen. He always believed that everything could be fixed and that he would be the person to fix it. He was half right: a lot *could* be done. Our hero would be Dr. Christopher Schlachta of St. Michael's Hospital. David's cancer was stage one and contained within the colon. It was operable and treatable, with a very encouraging prognosis.

David's father, Dick, wanted David to check into the Mayo Clinic Rochester, Minnesota. As an avid fan of Fox News, he had heard all about Canada's "socialist medicine," and he wouldn't trust a Canadian surgeon to remove a wart. David reassured his father that Dr. Schlachta was not only a pioneer in minimally invasive laparoscopic surgery but also among the best in North America — so good, in fact, that he was teaching his advanced techniques to American doctors.

On July 9, Dr. Schlachta removed eighteen inches of David's colon. The scarring from the surgery was so minimal that it looked as if someone had made three tiny pencil marks on his stomach. Postoperative recovery time was also reduced. In only a day or two, David was walking unassisted, and in a mere five days he was able to come home. That's when I *did* notice something odd about his behaviour. He was sitting contentedly in our family room watching *golf* — a sport he normally wouldn't even play because he found it so painfully slow. With a beatific look, he observed, "Golf is such an interesting game, isn't it?"

Two weeks later, David and I returned to the hospital to receive the postoperative pathology report. Though we were outwardly calm, when the doctor confirmed that David was clean, we both burst into tears, buckled at the knees, then started blubbering about how relieved *the kids* would be. I realized then how scared David had been, despite his bravado. Now his world righted itself. If he could have credited himself for the operation's success, I'm sure he would have. Ever afterward, when he recounted the story of his operation, the missing piece of colon grew longer — from eighteen inches to two and a half feet, amounting to half of an average colon.

The summer of 2004 became a joyous time for both of us.

We'd always had spectacular family vacations. Although travelling might have seemed like a busman's holiday for David, we took the four kids all over North America and Europe, to Africa and Australia. One summer we rented a farmhouse in the Burgundy region of France, then invited his Harvard friends, Lloyd and John Paul, with their young families to join us. Though they didn't feel they could afford a trip at that time, David delighted in being able to say, "No problem. I have enough frequent flier miles to get us all there for free." That was a magical summer, riding our bicycles to the local *boulangerie* for morning croissants, watching our kids have fun together, exploring the local markets, drinking wine, eating heartily, telling stories and laughing a lot.

The next summer, David drove our family in a nine-seater bus through Italy and Switzerland, with frequent stops to appreciate interesting places. This included an eight-hour detour in search of Great-Great-Grandfather Gustav's hometown in rural Switzerland. Wherever we went, David had read up on the history and culture, making him a very engaging and knowledgeable tour guide.

The vacation David and I took with Sarah and Becca three weeks after his surgery was one of our most carefree. Sarah's steel pan band — the Toronto All Star Steel Orchestra (TASSO) — was competing in the International Youth Music Festival in Aberdeen, Scotland, and David had been given permission to travel as long as he didn't lift any heavy bags. As Dr. Schlachta put it, "I don't want your hard work to ruin my good work."

David had replied, "I have a wife and two daughters as my sherpas."

We happily agreed to carry his bags and do all the heavy lifting.

Salmon Cupid, TASSO's Trinidad-born leader and composer, had always welcomed his students' families to participate in the band's activities, and David and I were big fans and supporters. TASSO's two dozen players, mostly from our local public school, would be competing as the only steel pan band against ninety-member conventional orchestras. TASSO brought the audience to its feet, dancing and clapping to Michael Jackson's "Don't Stop Till You Get Enough." The crowd kept TASSO on stage so long, the organizers had to intervene. TASSO won the competition. We were part of a very jubilant group of celebrating Toronto families.

Afterwards, the four of us toured Scotland and made a point of visiting the Edinburgh Festival. David loved festivals. He and Lloyd and John Paul had visited this one in 1978, the year David attended Sussex University, and each spring the three of them travelled to the New Orleans jazz festival. We immersed ourselves in everything Edinburgh had to offer — poetry readings, art shows, concerts, street theatre, and the military tattoo at Edinburgh Castle with its dazzling pyrotechnics. Our family especially loved *The Wife of Bath*, performed in rap at the Fringe festival by a Vancouver company. The kids considered its much-married heroine really cool without realizing she had been conceived six hundred years ago by Geoffrey Chaucer! The trip was the perfect antidote for what had been a very frightening time, and everything about it was marked with a luminosity born of our relief. The girls and I were simply enjoying a great vacation, but — as time would prove — seeds were germinating in David's fertile brain that would soon burst forth in a garden of colourful possibilities.

I had taken a leave of absence from my work in government after David received his diagnosis, and it was during this trip that I decided to stop working full-time to spend more time with our family. My work had been causing tension at home because I was unavailable much of the time or unable to talk about confidential issues with David. With so many projects on the go, David was always eager to know how to engage the government in supporting his latest venture. My reaction was to clam up. This curtailment of our dinner conversation was very frustrating for David. After he had been so ill, I felt a need to shift my priorities.

I discovered that the Ontario Trillium Foundation, a government agency granting millions of dollars annually to community-based programs, lacked a chair. I volunteered for the position, and was readily accepted. This gave me a leadership role in an organization that I loved, supporting projects that were important, but without the day-to-day responsibility of running the agency. I used to joke that the pay was lousy, but the benefits were great. It was a position and a lifestyle that suited me for the next few years.

While David's illness encouraged me to slow down, it had the opposite effect on him. His brush with mortality drove him to do more and more, faster and faster. He'd always overscheduled, but now he became ridiculously busy and increasingly impatient for everything to be done at once. I was used to seeing spurts of manic activity before, but now this behaviour became more intense and obvious to others.

We had a defining moment while attending a shiva for the mother of our friend Joanne Kates. A renowned food critic, Joanne had once described David as "a Cuisinart on high" — a metaphor that another friend, Chaviva Hosek, had extended with the phrase "and with no off switch." As a group of us talked about an acquaintance who had retired to Florida to play golf after a bout with cancer, and another who had quit work after a heart attack, David seemed unusually quiet. Suddenly, Joanne turned to him with a piercing stare, and asked, "David, what about you? You've had a nasty scare, and you're doing more of everything than ever before."

David paused, which was unlike him, being one of the fast-talking Pecauts with a quick and ready answer to everything. He even said, "Well ..." just like his more thoughtful, slower-talking mother and brother, surprising me almost as much as when I caught him watching golf. "I guess I might not have as much time as I thought to do all the things I need to do."

It was a simple, poignant answer.

———

When David's cancer had announced itself, he had been working on Pathways and the Strong Neighbourhoods Task Force. In the fall of 2004 — just three months after his surgery — he launched the project that he would later describe as the most important of his pro bono career.

Once again, David demonstrated the social problem that he intended to fix with a compelling story. It featured a single mother — I'll call her Janet — who had a severely asthmatic daughter. Janet had calculated the exact salary she could earn that would still entitle her to benefits under the Ontario Social Assistance Program. This also qualified her daughter for thousands of dollars in prescription drugs. The bank where Janet worked gave all its employees an automatic raise, putting her over the threshold for benefits. Since Janet wasn't allowed to refuse the increase, she had to quit her job and go back on full social assistance in order to afford her daughter's drugs.

Who benefited from this forced decision? Not Janet, not the bank, and not the Ontario Social Assistance Program.

David was particularly sensitive to income polarization because of his awareness of the wage gap between workers in global and in local industries. This was a discrepancy he'd found in every big city where he'd consulted, both in the manufacturing and knowledge sectors. What was true of Toronto was also true of New York and London. Income redistribution seemed to him fundamental to civic health.

In the debate leading up to *Enough Talk*, everyone around the table had agreed that dealing with poverty meant addressing Canada's thorny, convoluted, woefully out-of-date income security framework. Without its reform, programs like social housing were merely Band-Aid solutions. Federally, the structure hadn't been revised since the Pearson/ Trudeau era in the early 1960s. Provincially, the latest change had been negative — a dramatic reduction in social assistance rates by Mike Harris's Conservatives, after they'd been increased by David Peterson's Liberals and Bob Rae's NDP.

The Alliance partnered with St. Christopher House, a multi-service Toronto neighbourhood centre, to launch the Modernizing Income Security for Working-Age Adults task force, or MISWAA as it came to be known for lack of a simpler acronym. It was co-chaired by David and Susan Pigott, CEO of St. Christopher's House, with St. Christopher's providing pro bono staff, offices, and meeting space. Former CCG and BCG partner Jill Black had worked with David on many of his civic projects and took on the demanding role of project director, working alongside John Stapleton as research director and relying heavily on a large working group of experts on income security. The task force was comprised of fifty representatives of major employers, labour unions, policy institutes, universities, community organizations, advocacy groups, and foundations. A community reference group of low-income, working-age adults, some on welfare or disability insurance, was recruited to supply firsthand experience. All levels of government, including the Senate, were represented. Funding came from the Atkinson Charitable Foundation, the Laidlaw Foundation, the Law Foundation of Ontario, Maytree, TD Bank, and United Way of Greater Toronto, among others.

The aim of MISWAA was to provide a roadmap for modernizing income security to help families escape the welfare trap. Given the mix of poverty activists, think-tank economists, and strong right/left proponents, the group had its share of challenges when it came to finding common ground. Eventually, a number of principles became obvious to all. Everyone should have access to food, clothing, and shelter through a combination of personal resources, insured services like health care, and income security. A person who works a forty-hour week all year should not be living in poverty. And no one should be forced into a situation where he or she is financially better off by not working.

The establishment of these principles led to questions. What should the minimum wage be? What is the marginal tax rate on low-income people when they come off social assistance and go into the workforce? In other words, at what point is a person better off not working than working? How is the national child-benefit program working, and why isn't there a comparable provincial plan? How much does it cost per year for an individual to live with adequacy in Toronto?

That last question — *what is adequacy?* — allowed the low-income community reference group to contribute their hard-won experience. Members' answers ranged from $8,000 to $22,000, with $15,000 popping up with greatest regularity. This amount was also the income security that the federal government was providing for low-income seniors. Since it made no sense for someone working full-time all year to have an income less than the poorest senior, MISWAA chose $15,000 as its starting point for income replacement, though some task force members thought this was far too low.

MISWAA concluded that neither full-time work at Ontario's minimum wage nor social assistance alone was adequate for anyone living in Toronto. The big shocker came when the group tackled the question of marginal tax rate on low-income people when they came off social assistance to enter the workforce. It turned out to be over 100 percent for most, obliterating any economic value in working. This wasn't so much because of income taxes on wages, but because of the loss of such benefits as winter-coat allowance, subsidized housing, and paid prescriptions. As they discovered with Janet, those benefits were what really mattered.

As one task force member, an accountant, asked rhetorically, "Why would someone hit with a marginal tax rate of over 100 percent ever want to work?"

One of the low-income members from MISWAA's Community Reference Group replied, "Even if it doesn't make economic sense for me to have a job, there are other things that are important, like self-esteem and making a contribution to society."

David described this as a profound moment for the task force.

He personally had another of those moments when a young man whom he had invited to a steering meeting at the BCG offices didn't show up. Later, he discovered the security detail in BCG's office tower had refused to let him board the elevator because of his homeless appearance. David apologized profusely to the young man, who told him philosophically, "Look, it happens to me all the time."

MISWAA also concluded that the federal Employment Insurance (EI) program was completely broken, especially as it applied to the GTA.

All Canadian employees were supposed to have a safety net, but although 100 percent had to pay into EI, only 27 percent of Ontario residents and 22 percent of those in the GTA who lost their jobs could collect. The qualification for benefits depended on the number of hours worked, with that number being significantly lower in high unemployment regions like the Maritimes, where you could also seasonally go on and off Employment Insurance. In contrast, Toronto had a safety net with a hole so big that 78 percent fell through it. Then, to qualify for Ontario Social Assistance, the unemployed person had to spend his savings and liquidate his assets till he had only about $500 left, thereby stripping himself of everything that might keep him from spiralling downward. What made this a triple whammy was the fact that the 78 percent who fell through the hole were offered retraining that was infinitely inferior to the 22 percent who were caught by the EI safety net.

In 2006, MISWAA published a report entitled *Time for a Fair Deal: Modernizing Income Security for Working-Age Adults*. Its proposals were based on the understanding that a robust, just society can only be achieved by moving multiple levers — including minimum wage and EI reform, child care, health benefits, and skills-training programs. The report found that federal support of the poor had declined significantly relative to the provincial role, except when it came to seniors and children. Some of Ontario's social assistance burden had also been shifted onto municipalities, the level of government least able to afford it because of its heavy reliance on property taxes. This model was completely at odds with almost every other jurisdiction in North America.

The MISWAA report strongly recommended that the federal government end the EI program's regional bias. Losing your job in Ontario is just as tough as losing your job in Newfoundland. If you paid into EI, why should it matter what the employment rate in your area is? It might not even apply to your occupation, which might have a very high unemployment rate across the whole country.

The task force also believed that the federal government should provide a Basic Refundable Tax Credit for low-income, working-age adults, including those with disabilities, to be phased out when a household income reached $21,500 a year. This income supplement would reduce the penalties incurred by most households when moving from social assistance to earned income.

Prescription drugs, vision care, and dental coverage should be extended to low-income workers. Adults with serious dental problems were not only in pain, but were also restricted in the jobs they could take. To contain costs, the province should set up a dental clinic system and cap the benefit per person.

The report also recommended implementation of an Ontario child benefit program available for children of the working poor, not just for families on welfare as was currently the case. Ideally, this would match the federal system and grow over time. Low-income families could earn up to $21,480 and still collect child benefits, making it easier for them to leave social assistance. Taking children out of the welfare program would also dramatically lower its cost as a system, making it less of the lightning rod it had been in the 1990s. David personally felt that part of the difficulty in lining up votes for any war against poverty lay in framing it as a debate about welfare. The perception that it was a system supporting "lazy adults" had to be replaced with an understanding that most of the money went for the support of needy children.

To balance the needs of labour and employers, the report recommended the creation of an independent commission with representatives from both groups to review the minimum wage each year and to recommend increases when warranted. It also underlined the importance for the provincial government to enforce labour standards that would protect the large and growing temporary work force whose benefits were dramatically lower than those of employees with job security.

To gain traction for *Time for a Fair Deal*, MISWAA went for the big-bang approach. The *Globe and Mail* and the *Toronto Star* provided full-page ads for a letter to Prime Minister Stephen Harper and to Premier Dalton McGuinty, stating the need for income-security reform. It was signed by Mayor David Miller and mayors of other municipalities, all the business leaders on the task force, and others in the community.

*David with Naki
Osutei, Julia Deans,
Courtney Pratt, and
Genevieve Vallerand
at the 2007 Toronto
City Summit at
the Metro Toronto
Convention Centre.*

*DiverseCity
group photo at
the Canadian
Club for the
launch event,
January 2009.*

*David and Susan
Pigott, co-chairs,
launch the
landmark report
on Modernizing
Income Security
for Working
Age Adults
(MISWAA), May
2006.*

David at the launch of Enough Talk, *the first report of the Toronto City Summit Alliance, April 2003.*

David with Jane Stewart, Minister of Human Resources Development Canada, and Dominic D'Alessandro at the launch of the Toronto Region Immigrant Employment Council (TRIEC), September 2003.

David with Veronica Tennant and Jim Fleck at the Governor General Performing Arts Awards, September 2006.

With Amy, Becca, and Sarah on the red carpet for the Luminato opening gala in 2009.

With Joni Mitchell at her visual art exhibit, Green Flag Song, *at the CTV building on Queen Street West during Luminato 2008.*

Atom Egoyan speaks at the opening of Solar Breath | Light Air, *a tribute to David, in June 2010. The exhibit was curated by Atom and featured works by Michael Snow and Mani Mazinani.*

Luminato's founders share the stage at the 2006 opening.

Premier Dalton McGuinty joins Tony Gagliano, Lucille Joseph, and Helen Burstyn to celebrate Luminato's new hub in David Pecaut Square, June 2010.

David with his parents in the backyard of their Sioux City home in spring 1997, a few months before his mother's death on July 9.

David's fiftieth birthday celebration at our home in fall 2005. The Harvard friends and spouses reunite for the occasion.

Shelley, David, Stacey, and Dan. Their last time together at Dairymen's, summer 2008.

Coach David with Becca's rep basketball team, the North Toronto Huskies, in 2008.

Our family Christmas portrait, 2008.

Family photo at the wedding of our daughter Lauren to Matt Lawrence, in Malibu, October 10, 2009. Pictured L–R: Amy, Graham Smith, Helen, Matt, Lauren, David, Sarah, and Becca.

At the official City of Toronto opening and dedication of David Pecaut Square, April 8, 2010.

Once again, it was Team Toronto speaking up for itself and also for Canada's working poor.

Through negotiations with successive Liberal and Conservative federal governments, MISWAA received endorsement for its income-tax benefit for low-income workers, and a benefit for Canada's working poor became a fundamental part of the country's income-tax structure going forward.

On the provincial level, the task force worked aggressively with the government to establish a child-benefit program that would include the working poor. The group also gained consensus from Ontario's opposition parties so that when they attacked the budget as expected, they left the child-benefit section unchallenged.

The practical results of two years of concerted effort were substantial: provincial child benefits; workers' income-tax credits; dental clinics; labour enforcement standards. Much of this success stemmed from working effectively with all levels and stripes of government, and costing out each recommendation with federal and provincial financial departments as the process unfolded.

David felt elated. He knew that if poverty activists alone had demanded, yet again, an increase in benefits for the poor, or raising the minimum wage, it would have been politics as usual. But when business leaders who might be adversely affected by such changes added their voices, the debate was elevated to a new level. He also felt that the creating of a broad consensus from such a diverse group validated his own convening skills and strategies learned over the years.

As he summed up the experience, "MISWAA changed the landscape of income redistribution in Canada. It is probably the project of which I'm proudest in my whole career."

CHAPTER TWELVE

The Lunch That Launched
Five Thousand Dreams

T hey met as strangers, talked for a couple of hours, shook hands
on a deal to transform Toronto's cultural life, then ended up
calling each other brothers.

The time: a Saturday afternoon early in December 2003.

The venue: Yonge Street's Grano Restaurant, owned by Roberto
Martella.

The diners: David Pecaut and Tony Gagliano, executive chairman
and CEO of the St. Joseph Communications media empire. Both men
were big talkers, big dreamers, big fundraisers, and — most importantly
— big doers. The five thousand dreams they launched that day represents
the number of Canadian and international artists who have participated
in Luminato: The Toronto Festival of Arts and Creativity — the event
Tony and David envisioned over lunch that day.

Both men had been frustrated by the malaise into which the SARS
scare had plunged Toronto. Each was determined to do something
about it.

David had just finished chairing Toront03 with its groundbreaking
Rolling Stones concert in Downsview Park. His post-graduate degree had

been in the fine arts, and there was no form of creativity that he didn't enjoy. He loved music, from classical through jazz to rock and rap, which he thought to be the most innovative form to emerge in a generation. He even did a rap recruiting video for BCG, with the partners dressed in chains and do-rags, pronouncing BCG to be the coolest place to work. He was a prolific and eclectic reader of newspapers, magazines, non-fiction, and fiction, especially the short stories of his favourite writers, Alice Munro and Richard Ford. He loved theatre and film, visiting art galleries, and checking out every cultural exhibit or architectural wonder, new or old, wherever we travelled. For several years, we were co-owners of the Bay of Spirits, a native art gallery on Front Street. *Enough Talk*, published in April 2003, had earmarked arts and culture as activities vital to a dynamic city. Ever since David's discovery of the Edinburgh Festival in 1978, he had been mulling over how to create a magnificent multi-disciplinary cultural experience here in Toronto. For decades, a Luminato had been simmering in his psyche.

Tony Gagliano, one of ten children born to Italian immigrant parents, had been raised in a spirit of gratitude for the city that had allowed his family to prosper. As he described his dismay brought on by SARS, "Once you've seen the lights off, you know how important it is to keep them shining brightly." A virtuoso fundraiser for the Art Gallery of Toronto, he had been dreaming the same dream as David, but he had taken it one step further. He had commissioned Rocco Rossi, who had once worked with David at BCG, to do a feasibility study on international festivals: their budgets, their challenges, their impact. One of Rossi's promising conclusions was that Toronto's geographic location was ideal for hosting what could become North America's only big-time international multi-arts festival.

Tony had also discussed his burgeoning idea with William Thorsell, CEO of the Royal Ontario Museum and yet another big thinker skilled at taking grand ideas from concept to steel and concrete, as demonstrated by the ROM's $270-million renovation then in progress. It was Thorsell who advised him, "You should talk to David Pecaut. He gets things done."

And talk they did, for several hours at their December lunch at Grano — a late lunch, since David had just coached Becca's basketball team's practice. Even before the calamari arrived, it was clear that both Tony and

David shared a passion for culture and city building. To them, it was the most powerful way to define an urban centre locally and to burnish its reputation internationally. Both were sensitive to the snubs Toronto had received from World Fair and Olympics organizers after having invested enormous energy and considerable money into each bid. They wanted to establish something magnificent that Toronto could own independently and permanently, without having to beg yet another international body for the right to shine. They were pumped by the city's cultural aspirations as expressed through the physical transformation of its cultural institutions — the ROM, the Art Gallery of Ontario, the Royal Conservatory of Music, the Ballet Opera House, and the promise of a permanent home for the Toronto International Film Festival. They wanted to advertise Toronto's cultural dynamism — too long kept secret — to an appreciative world.

Tony's plan, tentatively labelled "The World in a City," called for combining the best Canadian and international artists the world had to offer. His ideas, passion, and commitment mirrored David's grand aspirations. The creative sparks flew. They both agreed it was time to go big or go home. And they both pressed for the festival to be an annual rather than a one-shot event to justify the herculean effort involved.

The kinship between the two men was immediate. Both were world-class optimists with the practical street smarts of effective entrepreneurs. Both were generous toward each other's ideas and harboured no hidden agendas. Both were warm and charismatic. Since both were also nonstop talkers, they must have developed the knack of listening, speaking, and eating at the same time.

When lunch was over, David extended his hand to Tony in a firm promise to carry the festival concept forward. As he later told me, "It's so remarkable in life to meet a partner like that and to make such a big commitment over one lunch."

Both Tony and David were savvy enough to understand that their first big step was to bring the arts community on board. They wanted its members to embrace the festival as a showcase for their talents, not resist it as a competitor for funding and audience. A series of discussions took place with Toronto's cultural czars, including, for starters: William Thorsell of the ROM, Piers Handling of the Toronto International Film Festival, Bill Boyle of Harbourfront Centre,

Matthew Teitelbaum of the Art Gallery of Ontario, Peter Oundjian of the Toronto Symphony Orchestra, Albert Schultz of the Young Centre for the Performing Arts, Kevin Garland and Karen Kain of the National Ballet of Canada, architect Bruce Kuwabara, filmmaker Atom Egoyan, and designer Bruce Mau.

Despite the importance of these cultural leaders to their own disciplines and to the city, they had rarely assembled in the same room to discuss common concerns and goals. The anticipated artistic sensitivities regarding turf were aired, often with zeal. Much skepticism was uncorked: *How could such a festival possibly work? Why should we support something that could eat into our grant money and sponsorship dollars? What do we get out of this?*

David was, by all accounts, at his best in finding common ground. Eventually, disgruntlement gave way to engagement, apprehension was replaced by appreciation of the big vision, and cynicism became cautious, then enthusiastic, optimism. A Festival Artistic Advisory Committee was created — an invaluable font of expertise and goodwill that allowed the idea to move forward.

"David was the consummate diplomat," noted Piers Handling. "Throughout all planning stages he was tireless, relentless, always on the phone, and always in a good mood. I was staggered by his ability to grapple with such a variety of issues at the same time."

"David was so patient with everyone's crazy ideas," remembers Karen Kain. "He loved the arts. After a ballet performance, he would write me emails about what he saw on stage that made me feel so fantastic. Such generosity and enthusiasm gave me courage."

Though Bill Boyle was initially a skeptic, he says, "You would go to David's festival meetings because you knew something would happen and you didn't want to miss it."

David and Tony, as festival co-chairs, along with their artistic advisors, soon hammered out the principles, both practical and aesthetic, that would frame the festival. It would take place for ten days in June when Toronto's weather should be warm enough for outside activities and before residents escaped to their cottages. It would feature the finest national and international artists. It would commission new works, especially those highlighting cross-disciplinary and cross-cultural collaboration. It would be accessible. It would include popular entertainment that would spill over the city into public parks and squares, showcasing the many natural and built attractions of Toronto. It would feature many free events, especially during the opening and closing weekends. It would reflect cultural and artistic diversity. It would burst — big, bold, and beautiful — onto the local and global scene, not introduce itself shyly with a promise to be better next time.

By the fall of 2005, meetings were happening every day. Tony also recalled many midnight phone calls in which David would ask, "Do you have two quick minutes?" then would end up claiming an hour. As ideas transformed into reality, Tony waved a red flag. "Look," he told David, "neither you nor I know how to run a festival. We can't go any further without somebody to work on this full-time."

In December 2005, Tony and David enlisted as interim CEO Lucille Joseph, a consulting colleague of David's who had worked with him on Career Edge and the Premier's Council, and who was already a committed volunteer. She and Julia Deans did an amazing job of putting together the necessary business infrastructure and recruiting board members.

"The first day I was on the job it was clear that the festival was weeks, even months behind schedule," said Lucille. "It stayed that way until just before we launched."

Lucille also provided a classic description of what it was like to attend a planning meeting. "A group would gather around a table. David would join us, usually late. He would expound on a new vision. People would get excited. A plan would start to emerge. David would leave, usually late for his next meeting, while the group continued. After a while a fog would settle in. Someone would ask, 'Why are we doing this?' Someone else would wonder, 'Is this remotely possible?' When you pushed through that fog, the vision would start to become your own, and a plan would emerge," she said. "Usually it would begin with David's making a phone call to whoever in the world was at the pinnacle of what you were doing. That person would also get excited. The enthusiasm of the group would rise till a new fog bank settled in, then cleared. After a couple of those cycles, a new venture would be born. The group would feel justly proud without realizing that in any single day, a number of those meteorological events would be happening all around David."

Funding for the festival was, of course, an ongoing concern. Tony and David estimated they would need a $3-million development budget plus $12 to $15 million a year to keep the festival running. For this, they were committed to finding new provincial and federal money rather than cannibalizing existing arts programs. Premier Dalton McGuinty and Liberal Finance Minister Greg Sorbara were quick to see the festival's potential. In November 2005, they granted $1 million seed money. The next fall, they added $1 million more. The federal Conservatives under Prime Minister Harper provided $1 million in 2008, the festival's second year, under a new program set up especially to support festivals. Ironically, the municipal government of Toronto — the festival's Cinderella — proved the hardest to engage. Their first-year support was limited to such things as putting up advertising flags and providing buses to transport groups of spectators from one core destination to another. Then, in the fall of 2008, the city committed $500,000 for a free waterfront spectacle staged by Cirque du Soleil.

Even before any government money materialized, "angels" began donating. The first was Charlie Baillie, former CEO of TD Bank Financial, who gave $100,000, establishing the benchmark for becoming a founding patron. Tony took the lead in signing up fifty others, including Michael Koerner, president of Canada Overseas Investments, and his wife, Sonja; David Young, president of The Hamilton Group, and his wife, Robin; Avie Bennett, chair of McClelland & Stewart; Margaret and Jim Fleck, committed philanthropists; and, of course, the Gagliano, Burstyn-Pecaut, and Joseph families, all of whom became known as Founding Luminaries. These were joined en route by Founding Corporate Luminaries such as TELUS, Bank of Montreal, Bank of Nova Scotia, and Manulife Financial. By the time the government money kicked in, the festival had raised $1.5 million in private and corporate funding, plus a promise of over $2 million in pro bono support.

The festival didn't find its chief corporate presenting sponsor until early in 2007. That's when Javier San Juan, CEO of L'Oréal Canada, signed on — with a flourish. As a Spanish ex-pat heading a French company whose Canadian subsidiary was based in Montreal, he underlined the festival's theme of unity in global diversity. It wasn't long before Javier and his wife, Connie, also became an integral part of the festival's growing family. In addition to generous sponsorship, L'Oréal became involved in contributing programming that celebrates beauty and creativity. In the festival's first year, Javier assigned Marcuso, a remarkable Montreal artist, to paint a sixty-foot mural in real time on a hotel wall, with spectators shouting suggestions as the work developed. In 2008, eclectic artist Pierre Maraval photographed one thousand Toronto women to be part of a head-turning exhibit at Brookfield Place.

David felt proud that festival funding reversed the international model in which government provided the core revenue with private sources sponsoring or donating as add-ons. The goal was for government support to shrink as the festival matured, becoming better able to attract more private funding.

The Toronto Festival of Arts, Culture and Creativity, as it had been incorporated, still lacked a distinctive name that would avoid the tongue-twisting acronym TFACC. It also required a website and a media strategy — needs that could be summed up as branding. David wanted to hold a competition among suitable agencies with an offer to pay the out-of-pocket costs of the winner. Though Tony found it hard to believe professionals would want to vie for pro bono work, David felt confident that the festival was already prestigious enough to attract candidates. Sure enough, four major agencies made substantial presentations. They chose MacLaren McCann, a Toronto firm with international connections, partly because of the enthusiasm of its creative director, Ian Mirlin.

Based on research with focus groups, Mirlin came back with the name LuminaTO, an invented word suggesting both light and enlightenment, with Toronto's nickname — TO — on the end. In street interviews, the twenty-to-thirty-year-old crowd made comments like, "Wow! That sounds edgy and electric and high tech." Older arts patrons remarked, "It's classical and Italian." In short — a winner! The tagline "The Toronto Festival of Arts and Creativity" was added like training wheels until Luminato could become so famous that if someone mentioned it in Paris or Sydney, people would know what it meant. Mirlin also came up with the metaphor of the city as a canvas and the festival as the paint to be colourfully splashed across it. The phrase "the paint on the canvas of the city" was one that David repeated over and over in his remarks.

One problem popped up: The website team discovered that a small Florida organization owned luminato.com. That URL was attached to a confusing website that seemed to indicate its owners were operating as a palm-tree-cutting business. An innocent inquiry purporting to be from an equally small Toronto group interested in purchasing the name produced a daunting warning: "What you are asking for could be quite expensive. I'm not sure you're going to want to buy it."

The Florida group named its princely sum: $2,000.

Of course, the relieved Toronto team snapped it up.

They were now facing the biggest dilemma of all: whether or not Luminato would be ready to launch in June 2007, only a year away. To seize the imagination of supporters, festival organizers had had to book events in full confidence that something fabulous was about to happen, without the money or the assurance that they could meet the schedule. A momentum had been building, but so had a legitimate concern. Again, it was Tony who articulated their greatest need: Where was the CEO superhero who would grab the reins and drive Luminato to its triumphant conclusion?

Executive recruiter Daniel Weinzweig had already zeroed in on Janice Price, CEO of Philadelphia's Kimmel Center for the Performing Arts and former vice-president of communications for New York's Lincoln Center. Born in Toronto, Janice was familiar with the Canadian scene from having headed up marketing for the Stratford Festival, as well as from stints with the Hummingbird Centre for the Performing Arts, Roy Thomson Hall, and Massey Hall.

When David contacted Janice by phone, she made it perfectly clear that she had no interest in returning to Canada. It took all of David's formidable powers of persuasion to get her to fly to Toronto one weekend in May 2006 for a preliminary interview. It was a rainy, gloomy day, and the churning grey skies of Toronto did not compare well to spring in sunny Philadelphia, where clouds of magnolias were already in bloom.

Janice met with David, Tony, and Lucille in our sunroom — David's favourite room in the house and his preferred weekend meeting space. She had expected to encounter three well-intentioned amateurs, wearing their dreams on their sleeves, oblivious to the risk and complexity of creating a festival. Instead, she found a trio of audacious entrepreneurs, with branding and bookings in place, backed by an internationally renowned group of cultural leaders, funded by government, corporate sponsors, and private angels. During the interview, which stretched to three hours, Janice allowed herself to be swept up in the collective dream. In Luminato, she saw an opportunity to employ and expand her own talents to create something unique — a performing arts festival without walls. To her surprise, she also discovered that even after ten years in the United States she still cared about showcasing Toronto in a way that would thrill its citizens and charm the world.

As Janice's cab pulled out of our driveway, David jogged beside her open window, still piling on ideas, whipping up her enthusiasm to match his own.

After a number of intense follow-up phone calls, Janice signed on as Luminato's CEO. "David was the Pied Piper. He articulated his vision and we all followed," said Janice. "He had an incredible capacity to see the big picture, not just from his own point of view but from others' as well."

This confirmation was the signal Tony and David needed to press the button that would ignite the fuse that would light up Toronto for ten days in June of 2007.

As it turned out, Janice was exactly what Luminato needed to make the festival happen.

During my own first encounter with her, I was impressed by how fast her mind worked and how well she covered so many bases at once; however, it took me a couple of festivals of watching from the sidelines to realize how difficult her task was and how truly talented she was at it. She herself described her job as "playing chess in 3-D." Janice was also perceptive about balancing Tony and David, involving each in complementary ways — who should introduce at each event and what role the other should play. An extreme extrovert, Janice was also the right balance to Lucille, who was quieter and a good listener. It was the four of them working so harmoniously that made Luminato the incredible success it became.

The whole Burstyn-Pecaut family loved Luminato from start to finish. With some of David's projects, the girls and I had felt as if we were competing for his time, but we all experienced ourselves as part of the rich fabric of Luminato. We envisioned it together. We talked about it at the dinner table. We bounced ideas off one another, and everyone in the family had a say. Luminato became a running conversation as we worked and travelled and lived our lives. It was an idea that kept building and layering as it took shape over the years. The festival spirit was upon all of us, and that was also true of the Gaglianos. Tony and his wife, Lina, and their children became an integral part of our lives. It was as if Luminato were a joint family project.

Luminato was officially launched on June 2, 2007. The timing coincided with the official opening of Daniel Libeskind's renovation of the ROM, and the decision to launch the two in tandem provided yet another fine example of collaboration across the arts. Everyone who had worked to bring both projects to triumphant completion was there, in a program that combined the pomp of officialdom with the exuberance of a street party, swelling out in waves from ROM's Bloor Plaza. It was a *son et lumière* to remember, with a spectacular show of coloured images sweeping across the prismatic facade of the ROM's Michael Lee-Chin Crystal, featuring a concert of various pop, classical, rock, jazz, opera, folk, and gospel musicians. An estimated fifty thousand people attended the free performance. Shivers of excitement shot up and down our spines as the magnitude of this event unfolded.

Over the next ten days, Luminato rolled out its one hundred events seamlessly — or that's how it appeared to those of us with one foot behind the scenes and the other in front, watching this bold vision become a spectacular reality. It was incredible to David that this was actually happening after four years of listening to naysayers: *You won't get enough money. You won't get world-class artists. You won't get the audience. You won't be able to justify the expense.* All that negativity had only made David redouble his efforts.

One of the greatest lures for the arts community had been the commissioning of new work, especially pieces that boldly crossed the lines between disciplines and cultures. Peter Oundjian, the TSO's artistic director, had suggested that he and his cousin, Eric Idle of Monty Python fame, produce a comic oratorical version of the movie *Life of Brian* as a commissioned collaboration between the symphony and Luminato. This became the hilarious *Not the Messiah,* which premiered at Luminato, then toured the world. David was delighted when the production not only wowed our daughter Amy but also converted her and her friends into symphony and opera lovers.

David had similar high hopes for the public art Luminato installed across the city. Once intrigued by, say, Max Streicher's ghostly and gigantic four horses, floating over the Great Hall of Union Station, or William Forsythe's magical *Scattered Crowd* of cascading white balloons festooning Toronto-Dominion Centre, people who were once intimidated by art galleries might be more inclined to venture inside.

Don Shipley, former director of the prestigious World Stage Theatre series at Harbourfront, knew that American composer Philip Glass was writing music to accompany the recorded poems of Leonard Cohen's *Book of Longing,* described as playful, erotic, and meditative. This also became a co-commissioned premiere performed by indie, rock, and new music artists that then toured the world. Another major coup for Luminato and Toronto!

Atom Egoyan, a celebrated Canadian filmmaker of Armenian descent, had expressed the desire to collaborate with Kutlug Ataman, a visual artist from Turkey, reflecting back on the Armenian genocide. They created *Auroras/Testimony,* twin videos, powerful and controversial, opposed but conjoined, dazzling in the originality of their style and the horror of their content. The production later travelled to the Istanbul Biennial. As a special bonus, Atom became a treasured family friend.

Another collaborative triumph was *Vida!* featuring the Lizt Alfonso Cuban dance company, a fiery world premiere for which producer David Mirvish covered most of the costs of development. It became the subject of a Gemini-nominated film directed by former National Ballet star Veronica Tennant, who also became a close friend.

A series of public discussions, called Illuminations, gave festival fans an opportunity to hear conversations with Philip Glass and Leonard Cohen, along with provocative interviews with literary figures like Gore Vidal.

One highlight of Luminato's many free concerts, installations, and events strewn across Toronto in 2007 was *Pulse Front*, the world's largest interactive light sculpture, co-produced with Harbourfront Centre and conceived by Montreal-Mexican artist Rafael Lozano-Hemmer. When members of the public put their hands on one of twenty onsite controls linked to computers, each heartbeat was transmitted to one of twenty searchlights sweeping the skies over the waterfront. It thrilled David to see all these pulsing searchlights, so intimately connected to each individual yet lighting up the firmament. He thought it exactly caught the spirit of Luminato, transmitting Toronto's heartbeat to the rest of the world.

For ten glorious days, our family immersed itself in the panorama.

The inaugural Luminato featured over 1,300 local and 214 international artists performing at over thirty venues across downtown Toronto. More than 1,035,000 people, local and visitors, swarmed to its events, featuring ten world premieres, including six commissioned or co-commissioned works.

"At The Boston Consulting Group, there was one time when you never wanted to be around David. That would be at the end of a project. You would be exhausted. The whole team would be exhausted, and you would want a day to clean up your papers and go out to lunch and perhaps even leave early. You would know that David was down the hall at his desk, and that he'd be bored, and that he'd be thinking about the next big thing he'd like to do," recalled Lucille. "He would wander down the hall, everyone would duck, but sooner or later he would end up in your office with a great idea, telling you, 'It's going to be so much fun, and so easy to do! I can't wait to get started,' and you would feel yourself being drawn in. Still, I have to say, that the times David did drop into my office produced some of the best experiences of my life, and I wouldn't have missed them for the world."

———

From 2007 to 2010, Luminato showcased 5,760 artists, over 80 percent of whom were Canadian. Thirty-seven new works were commissioned or co-commissioned, with thirty-one of those also touring Canada and the world.

Each year Luminato reaches about one million people. On average, 140,000 tourists participate in Luminato, and 75 percent of the tourists attending ticketed events report that they came to Toronto especially for the festival, generating $553 million in visitor expenditures.

Yet when David talked about what Luminato meant to him, he spoke mostly about things that can't be quantified. One was his very special relationship with Tony Gagliano — the passion they shared for the arts, the respect they had for each other. He was grateful for how the leaders of the various arts communities joined in supporting a shared vision. He appreciated the commitment of the Ontario and federal governments, and the other corporate and individual angels who had the confidence and the faith to invest in a big idea. He felt fortunate to have had the professional talent of people who knew how to build solidly from the ground up. He felt privileged, he felt proud, he felt blessed to see the city light up with Luminato's special brand of magic, and to know that the same enlightenment would be happening for years to come.

CHAPTER THIRTEEN

The Absolut David

D avid was fascinated by the ability of San Diego to transform itself from a naval base with low-wage retail jobs and some tourism into a world leader in technology research in only a few years. This happened from 1980 to 1995 under Richard Atkinson, chancellor of the city's University of California. Mindful of the faculty's electronics and biomedical expertise, Atkinson mandated sociologist Mary Walshok to promote this in-house research to a wider audience.

Walshok began by telling grads in the business community, "We appreciate your donations, but what we really need are your Rolodexes. Perhaps you own a car dealership or are in retail, but surely every one of you knows somebody at General Electric or Hitachi or in venture capital who would be interested in your alma mater's exciting technology."

Walshok then began matching up businessmen to researchers, one of whom was Irwin Jacobs, a physics professor who had developed innovative cellphone technology. Though Jacobs had shown no interest in marketing it, Walshok introduced him to a grad who knew the top venture capitalists at Kleiner Perkins. After a chain reaction of contacts, Jacobs founded Qualcomm Incorporated, now a company with more than 13,000 American patents for wireless technologies, licensed by more than 180 telecommunications manufacturers worldwide.

Using the same strategy, the University of California attracted the Scripps Institute of Oceanography for marine science research, as well as the Salk Institute for Biological Sciences. These initiatives boosted private donations from $15 million to $50 million annually, allowing the faculty to expand by nearly 50 percent and enrollment to double. Most importantly, San Diego became a leading centre for intellectual property and research.

In David's keynote speech to the first City Summit in June 2002, he had described global companies as the driving force of urban economies and emphasized the GTA's need to compete to attract them. This theme was strengthened and expanded in the 2003 publication *Enough Talk*.

The TCSA founded the Toronto Region Research Alliance (TRRA) in September 2005, largely based on the San Diego model. A non-profit organization funded by all levels of government, the TRRA was co-chaired by Gordon Nixon, CEO of the RBC Financial Group, and Dr. John Evans, founder of the MaRS Discovery District, where TRRA established an office. Ross McGregor, who was very involved in the founding of the organization, was recruited as its CEO. The TRRA's mandate was to unite the technological, educational, medical, and financial institutions of the Golden Horseshoe in a concerted effort to expand and attract research facilities. If San Diego could do it, why not the Golden Horseshoe? As David noted, our region had a much deeper science and technology capability, backed by a far greater global financial and business community. For David, this was an opportunity waiting for him to make it happen.

TRRA started with the awareness that this region, in which over 35 percent of Canadian research and development was concentrated, had not been receiving anywhere close to its fair share of federal investment. While the National Research Council had some thirty centres, there wasn't one in the Golden Horseshoe. Its last major initiative — the NRC's National Institute for Nanotechnology — should have come to Toronto, where the experts were located, but it went to Edmonton because the government of Alberta was willing to fund it, while Ontario was not. Making matters worse, the NRC then proceeded to hire many of its senior staff from Toronto.

TRRA's first objective was to stand up for the Golden Horseshoe in attracting public, private, and corporate research capital. On learning, post SARS, that the federal government planned to locate its infectious-disease agency entirely in Winnipeg, TRRA persuaded Paul Martin's Liberals, with Carolyn Bennett as Minister of State for Public Health, to spread some of the research to the University of Toronto and to McMaster University Medical Centre. TRRA also supported successful bids for provincial and federal funding for University of Waterloo's Centre for Quantum Computing, and for locating the CANMET Materials Technology Laboratory at McMaster Innovation Park. CANMET, with the world's most powerful quantum microscopes, became southern Ontario's first major federal lab.

TRRA then took aim at global targets. Through BCG's pro bono research, the TRRA team had discovered twenty technologies in which the Golden Horseshoe was a world leader. Based on this research, TRRA demonstrated to a Japanese company that this region was unique in providing all necessary capabilities for developing its printing inks. It also persuaded AGFA, one of the world's top medical imaging companies, to almost triple its Waterloo facility at a time when AGFA was closing labs around the world.

One of David's gnawing concerns was Ontario's lack of early-stage venture capital for supporting technological initiatives. Most of what did exist was passive, whereas David knew, from his global experience, that only active venture capital, where investors were involved in attracting talent and promoting innovation, succeeded in moving beyond the early developmental stages. Of greatest importance were "life cycle" investors who acted as angels during the first stage, with the intention of making second-, third-, and fourth-stage investments to emerge as major shareholders when the enterprise bore fruit. To fill this vacuum, the TRRA team convinced the province that it should be first in and last out when funding promising ventures. While the government's money would be at greater risk, it would provide the necessary incentive to attract private-sector investment to grow the enterprise.

One of the TRRA's most frustrating failures highlighted the need to update government policy to compete globally for high-tech investment. In 2005, Xerox wanted to establish a billion-dollar North American export plant to exploit an exciting new technology for making colour toner at twice the output for half the cost, with a dramatically smaller environmental footprint. As well as generating over a billion dollars in exports, all of the plant's roughly four hundred jobs would be white-coat.

Oakville already had one of Xerox's most successful laboratories, turning out fifty patents a year. In addition, Xerox had built a successful pilot plant for toner adjacent to this Oakville facility. Their Oakville people understood the technology, and Xerox owned the land for a new plant to locate there. This should have been a slam dunk.

TRRA created a working group with Ottawa, Ontario, and the Oakville lab to make sure this would happen. In Phase 1, Ontario was competing against four or five American states. Eventually, the field narrowed to Ontario versus New York, the traditional home of Xerox.

As negotiations proceeded, David grew concerned that Ontario didn't have the right policy levers to attract technology investment. To begin with, Ontario didn't allow development charges for new industrial facilities to be rebated. This made sense on the provincial level since it prevented Oakville from, say, stealing a company from Barrie by rebating development charges; however, it was a huge stumbling block in attracting a billion-dollar global facility to Canada. At the same time, the Ontario sales tax added 8 percent to everything that would be used for manufacture in the facility.

New York State agreed to rebate 100 percent of the sales tax to Xerox, while the local community would rebate 100 percent of the development charges. A billion-dollar export plant that should have come to Ontario went to New York because it offered $10 to $15 million in incentives.

David thought this was crazy. The TRRA team requested that Ontario create a tool kit offering high-tech companies the same kind of incentives available to automotive companies. Considerable progress has since been made in that area.

In summing up David's personal contribution to TRRA, Chaviva Hosek, a TRRA director and CEO of the Canadian Institute for Advanced Research, commented, "In his passion to make things better, David generated more ideas per square second than anybody I ever knew. I sometimes wondered, 'Does David Pecaut have a dimmer switch?'"

Despite David's overlapping work with TRRA, MISWAA, the Strong Neighbourhoods Task Force, Luminato, and his clients at BCG, he made a real effort after his surgery to free up more time for our family, which we all agreed was the best gift he could give us, and himself.

Sports had always been one of our family's shared activities. The first thing David had requested on settling into our home was a basketball hoop over our garage. Since we were a family of all girls, David considered setting it lower than the regulation ten feet. Our handyman was adamant about the height of the hoop, noting, "Where there are girls, there are going to be boys." He was right. All our girls turned out to be excellent players, and they would have been insulted to be handicapped. That hoop was in constant use through the years by our kids and their friends. Often it was just David shooting baskets on his own.

David coached school basketball teams for both Sarah and Becca. After Becca's talent earned her a position as a rep player in the North Toronto Huskies League, David became an assistant coach of that team, and then its main coach — an activity he continued, full-throttle, until a year before his death. David knew everything about basketball, and he was a gifted teacher. The girls on his team were devoted to him, and even today young women tell me about their wonderful memories of Coach David, as do their parents, who were a welcome part of the team dynamic.

"I always loved having my dad coach because he never yelled or lost his temper," says Becca. "He always encouraged us to play smart, and when we lost, he made it into a great learning opportunity."

Sarah excelled at volleyball, with David enthusiastically cheering from the sidelines. He also co-coached a soccer team for Sarah and Becca. Because no one in Sioux City had ever played the game when he was a kid, he didn't know much about it. Nevertheless, when he heard that our Moordale neighbourhood league needed a coach, he pored over some soccer manuals at our kitchen table, then asked our friend Henry Vehovec, who was a seasoned coach, for advice on drills and strategy. Always a quick study, David become an overnight expert, then coached his team to one victory after another.

Our girls knew that whenever a team needed coaching, their dad would be there for them. "He learned the rules of soccer just so he could coach our soccer team, but his greatest love was basketball," says Becca.

He loved playing it, he loved coaching it, and he loved watching it. Every year he purchased four season tickets for the Toronto Raptors, and we'd make each game a social event for friends and family. For those who didn't know anything about the game, David would happily explain the action on the court as it was happening.

David had always treated our daughters' friends as if they were family. Lauren's friends had taken to calling him "David Encyclopedia" because he knew so much about so many things — from Buddhism to jazz, from his claim that babies were born with perfect pitch to the Mathletes cheer he had learned in high school. It was sometimes dangerous to ask him a simple question because of the detail and depth of his answers, which often included a list of books and well-researched articles recommended for further reading. This came in handy for school projects, sometimes inspiring weekend field trips to art galleries and book launches.

Music was another of our family's shared passions. I remember David playing at our living room piano with Sarah on his lap, so small she couldn't sit up, but still managing to sing along. It was the same with Becca. When she was only three, you could hum the opening notes of any Disney tune, and she could identify not only the song but also the character who had sung it.

For my fiftieth birthday, barely three months after David's surgery, he staged a big celebration for me at the Eglinton Grand. Though barely recovered and functioning at what he described as 80 percent of his usual energy level, he threw himself 100 percent into party planning. He billed the two-hundred-person celebration as "Helen's Bat Mitzvah," and invited the Toronto All-Stars steel pan band, in which Sarah and Becca played, to perform opening numbers. For David's fiftieth birthday a year later, the girls and I converted our house into a jazz cafe and, on the recommendation of our friend Michael McAdoo, engaged rising Canadian jazz star Dione Taylor to perform. Uncharacteristically, David insisted that his party be not too big, so I billed it as "50 for 50" — fifty of our closest friends celebrating David's fiftieth birthday. The number attending was a little more than advertised, but David forgave the overrun because he didn't want to exclude people he loved from such a special celebration. Guests flew in from all over the continent to be with us.

As well as enjoying concerts, David and all his girls loved to dance. And since David always made certain our house was full of music, those speakers I had installed in every room ensured that we were always hearing the same songs, which offered spontaneous dance opportunities.

David thrived on being the only male in a household of women, which included a succession of female dogs. He found girl talk captivating. Ours was a family that knew about fashion, and while David had no sense of style whatsoever, he was curious about its role in our lives. He loved Amy's ability to spot trends. She decorated her room in leopard before anyone knew what a big fashion statement that would become, then she plastered her walls with Absolut vodka ads before *The Absolut Vodka Advertising Story* was published. She even started a series of 3D Absolut wall plaques as part of a school art project, including *Absolut David* — a mounted bottle with a pair of his glasses perched on its neck, unfashionably dressed in a purple tie and black bathrobe. Sarah later picked up on this Absolut theme to create a wall plaque for each of her sisters.

Nothing feminine caused David to shy away. When Sarah came into puberty, I remember seeing her perched on his lap, carrying on a very intimate conversation that seemed natural to both of them. David always said he didn't need any boys since he received everything he ever wanted from his girls. He sometimes mused about writing a book titled *A Martian on Venus,* about life in an all-female household.

CHAPTER FOURTEEN

Greening Greater Toronto

In February 2007, the TCSA held its third City Summit. Called Making Big Things Happen, it was a packed two-day affair at the Metro Toronto Convention Centre.

The TCSA had proven itself to be a can-do organization with an impressive record in tourism, immigration, youth, education, housing, income security, and technology. Five hundred participants were expected. Six hundred and thirty showed up. David even had CEOs calling him at the last minute begging him to shoehorn in just one more. Word was out, both in the media and on the street. The Summit was a don't-miss happening.

All the major political parties and levels of government attended, and many had speaking parts. Keynote experts addressed items still on the TCSA to-do list — the green agenda, transportation, and the need for leadership diversity. Despite the size of the crowd, organizers invoked the roundtable concept by dividing into groups of eight or ten. As David went from table to table eavesdropping, he was struck by conversations like the one between Domenic D'Alessandro, then CEO of Manulife, a worldwide top-five life insurance company, and a transportation advocate who rode her bike to work every day. To the obvious surprise of the transit/bike advocate, Domenic agreed that road tolls were an appropriate way to raise transit funding, since the last thing he wanted was for his employees to be commuting on the QEW in their SUVs, adding to global warming, taking forever, and arriving stressed.

At a nearby table, a civic worker was baiting another CEO, "Well, we know you guys like the fact that all of us have different standards for pollution. That lets you play us off one against another, by choosing to go with the municipality that has the lowest standard."

The CEO's response was just as heated: "That's totally crazy! It's exactly the opposite. A universal standard across the region would save us money and lower costs."

Waste disposal was another hot topic. Workers actually involved in the shipping of waste were incensed that much green-box material was being dumped in landfills because the city lacked recycling options to repurpose it. Though this was well known to insiders, it was news to the general public until the *Toronto Star* later ran a series of exposés.

These meaningful exchanges confirmed for David an appetite for civic engagement, along with the major role the TCSA could play in convening people of different backgrounds for exciting conversations about matters everyone cared about.

Two strong initiatives came out of the 2007 Summit. The first was Greening Greater Toronto (GGT), which David co-chaired with Eva Ligeti, executive director of Clean Air Partnership, and Mike Pedersen, Group Head, Corporate Operations of TD Bank Financial Group. Previously, city environmentalists had bypassed business leaders to direct their efforts at government. As with all David's projects, GGT crossed those boundaries to bring together all interested parties, along with provincial and city representatives. The goal of GGT's forty-five-member task force, with its four working groups, was to build upon existing environmental efforts to make the GTA the greenest city region in North America.

Through 2007 into early 2008, a pro bono BCG team put together a deep and thorough analysis of the GTA's environment, including air and water quality, greenhouse gases, and the use of green space: How much CO_2 was being produced from private car use versus public transit? How much from commercial buildings versus public ones? The biggest surprise was the discovery that buildings were worse polluters than cars. Commercial and public buildings created 31 percent of greenhouses gases, with residences accounting for an additional 23 percent, pushing the total to 54 percent. In contrast, personal vehicles created 21 percent, with commercial and public vehicles accounting for 15 percent, for a total of 36 percent.

The analysis of waste and its diversion also produced some unexpected results. While the GTA's focus was on residential recycling, especially targeting single-family dwellings, these accounted for only one-third of waste, as opposed to the two-thirds that was non-residential. Of the residential waste, 39 percent was being diverted. Of the non-residential waste, only 18 percent was being diverted, with the remaining 82 percent being dumped as landfill. Of that amount, 31 percent was paper, which is recyclable. In other words, 20 percent of all GTA's landfill waste was non-residential paper!

Greening Greater Toronto, based on BCG's startling findings and the work of hundreds of task force and working group members, was published in June 2008. It established five clear goals: reduction of greenhouse gases, improved air quality, improved water quality, more efficient waste management, and sustainable land use. It also envisioned a time when the GTA's beaches would always be open, its rivers teeming with aquatic life, its tree canopy extended, its greenbelt protected, its air pure, and its waste reduced through maximum recycling.

The GGT report was packed with detailed, comparative research. Toronto's greenhouse gas emission was better than the GTA's, and the GTA's was better than the San Francisco Bay Area's. In terms of waste diversion, Toronto and the GTA were doing well in comparison to New York, but trailing behind the Greater Vancouver Area and Edmonton.

The report identified a number of initiatives that should be undertaken in cooperation with active green groups and other partners. The first was to help drive a large-scale retrofit of GTA commercial and public buildings, our greatest consumers of energy and our worst producers of greenhouse gases. For an average building, a retrofit could achieve energy reductions of 10 to 50 percent. For example, Oshawa's improvements to its city hall and other municipal buildings reduced greenhouse gas emissions energy costs by about 50 percent, for annual savings of $500,000.

The GTA's largest landlord is the Ontario government, followed by the Royal Bank, then the federal government. The Bank of Montreal and the TD Bank are also major real estate holders. All have now invested large sums to retrofit, building by building, directly creating an estimated five thousand jobs per year and indirectly creating even more. By starting early, Toronto was also positioning itself as a major exporter of green technology. This was demonstrated by a visit from a fact-finding New York delegation, representing Mayor Michael Bloomberg, faced with the same issues.

As often happens with innovative ideas, unexpected challenges popped up. Most commercial tenants in Toronto (and North America) pay their own energy and utility costs. This meant that landlords did not believe they would benefit from retrofit investments. GGT created working groups composed of major commercial landlords, tenants, and technical service providers. The tenants quickly made it clear that they would not remain in buildings that were not retrofit and that they were willing to work with their landlords to improve energy use, thus transforming the landlords into willing partners. GGT also helped to develop a green lease amendment, allowing landlords to gain their tenants' permission to recoup energy savings brought about by their investments.

David was especially excited about encouraging large corporate and public clients to use green technologies suppliers. At the Ontario Centres of Excellence annual conference that year, there were some fifty organizations representing over $50 billion in procurement power. Greening Greater Toronto seized the opportunity to showcase a pre-vetted group of twenty green providers, who pitched everything from clean photocopying to water use. The green companies declared this to be their most successful event ever.

Another major GGT initiative was the creation of the Greening Canada Fund. GTA companies could pay for emission reduction by buying offset credits from schools, public housing, hospitals, and other institutions. This would position Toronto as a North American leader by anticipating legislation making carbon neutrality mandatory and providing other gains from carbon reduction, allowing us to benefit from dollars that would otherwise chase international offset sellers.

As always, David kept actively in touch with every phase of the GGT operation. As his co-chair, Mike Pedersen, stated, "David had the drive of the Energizer Bunny, a head the size of a watermelon, and a heart to match."

I cite this compliment with a sense of wonder, because even while David was pouring energy into Greening Greater Toronto and his other civic projects, even while he was advising billion-dollar corporations, he was fighting a tough personal battle against staggering odds, and one he would lose.

———————

Following David's surgery, he was supposed to visit St. Michael's Hospital for routine checkups every six months. After cancelling one such appointment, he discovered symptoms that gave him a heart-stopping reason to believe his cancer might have returned. An examination in December 2007 turned up "suspicious matter" in the colorectal area. Though David and I tried to keep our anxiety private over Christmas while we awaited results, Lauren, our oldest daughter, later told me she guessed something was wrong because we were not our lively selves. Instead, we were quiet and tense, and held hands in a white-knuckle way that suggested more than comfortable affection.

David received the dreaded report on January 7. He had colorectal cancer, confirming our worst fears, and even exceeding them, since this was a different kind of cancer in a place difficult to detect. Perhaps it had been there for a while. Perhaps David's missed appointment had been critical. At first, David was angry with his medical team for not insisting that he take his checkup, but everyone who knew David recognized that missing appointments was a pattern with him. Our dentist later shocked me when she told me that, despite repeated reminders, she hadn't seen him in six years!

Because David's cancer was so difficult to diagnose, a doctor at St. Mike's took a needle biopsy of the lymph nodes in David's groin. It, too, came back positive, indicating that the cancer had moved into David's system. His first diagnosis had been stage one, meaning contained, treatable, and curable. Because this new cancer had spread, the diagnosis was now an automatic stage three — uncontained, treatable, but not necessarily curable. We were fighting a new and deadlier battle.

In retrospect, seemingly simple events took on the aspect of milestones. I remember David and I sitting around our sunroom table with writer Val Ross, a beloved friend who had been diagnosed with brain cancer. She and David were teasing each other — not frivolously or sadly, but ironically — about who would die first. As fate decreed, Val was struck down in February 2008, age fifty-seven. Many times over the next two years, David would refer to this conversation with Val as he slid down his own slippery slope to the same inevitable end.

Val's death was heartbreaking — a real body blow, previewing for me what it would be like to lose David.

CHAPTER FIFTEEN

"All You Need Is to Be the One"

David's last major pro bono undertaking was DiverseCity: The Greater Toronto Leadership Project. This was the second big initiative to come out of the 2007 City Summit and was created by the TCSA and Maytree. Despite the return of his cancer, David insisted on co-chairing this too, along with Maytree president Ratna Omidvar. The aim of this group was to make the GTA's leadership as diverse as its population.

In his support for DiverseCity, David cited the findings of Scott Page in his book *The Difference: How the Power of Diversity Creates Better Groups, Firms, Schools, and Societies.* Page established that if you pit a group with average ability but a high degree of cognitive diversity against a homogenous group with superior ability, the average but diverse group will outperform the superior group in problem-solving 99 percent of the time. Though Page did not necessarily define "diverse" in terms of cultures, David considered the correlation to be an obvious one.

DiverseCity was introduced by David to the city's corporate and non-profit leadership at a January 2009 Canadian Club luncheon. When David looked out at the audience of six hundred, he was grateful to see many representatives of different backgrounds, along with CEOs like Gord Nixon of the Royal Bank and Ed Clark of the TD Bank Financial Group. He described DiverseCity as an opportunity to tap into the skills of a diverse yet proven leadership — the approach chosen during meetings with visible minority communities who wished to bypass the dated idea of affirmative action to stress the economic and social benefits of inclusion.

One highly successful initiative undertaken by Maytree was DiverseCity on Board, in which a roster of people from visible minorities were matched with appropriate public boards, such as that of the Science Centre and GTA hospitals. In the first eight months, well over two hundred matches were made.

This gave birth to another program — the DiverseCity Voices speakers' bureau. Media such as the CBC, the *Globe and Mail*, and the *Toronto Star* agreed to train members to talk about their expertise, not in problems arising from diversity but in, say, stem-cell research. As an offshoot, the media trainers began using these experts on the national news and quoting them in articles.

Like TRIEC, Career Edge, and Career Bridge, DiverseCity Fellows was a mentorship program, this time for training candidates as city leaders. Each year, twenty-five promising people reflecting regional as well as ethnic diversity would be chosen. They would be given twelve months of leadership training, including networking, feedback, and face time with executives. These Fellows would then use their new skills as a team to create city-building projects and to train others in their communities.

In its third-year report, DiverseCity was able to point to an 8 percent increase of visible minorities in GTA leadership — an encouraging start, though still far from fair representation. The figures are impressive: more than a thousand new leaders were introduced to places of influence and power. But perhaps more important, this program has legitimized the conversation about diversity in leadership, something David emphasized when he addressed the business leaders at that Canadian Club lunch event.

David's interest in diverse leadership and mentorship were combined in the creation of the Emerging Leaders Network of promising young civic leaders working collaboratively on challenges facing the region. When it was founded in 2006, the ELN started as a group of fifty mid- to senior-level executives working in the private, public, and non-profit sectors. Since then, the network has grown to more than five hundred members.

While all this was happening publicly, David was fighting his colorectal cancer with every physical, mental, and emotional resource he had. And with the latest research. And with the finest medical experts. Hadn't his mother survived a cancer that all her doctors had predicted would kill her in five months? She had been a one-percenter — the one person in a hundred who had beaten the odds. David's mantra became: "All you need is to be the one."

Fortunately, many of the best medical specialists were located in Toronto. Dr. Christine Brezden-Masley, an oncologist at St. Michael's Hospital, was an excellent fit for David — very smart, aggressive, innovative, and just as insistent as David on finding a cure, though she knew his chances were slim. She was also quick to provide records for other doctors or get David the latest research findings touching on his case, since he was reading everything he could, following up on every recommendation, and having many medical consultations every week.

BCG responded with exceptional generosity to David's illness by giving him a whole case team. It included Tony Nimeh, a BCG consultant who was also a doctor, assigned to work full-time with David. When David and I flew to the U.S. to see specialists, Tony travelled with us as our knowledge broker. He wrangled appointments, asked all the technical questions, interpreted the findings for us, and followed up every session with a detailed slide deck summarizing the outcomes and options. Though Team David hit many dead ends, Tony helped us discover Dr. Leonard Salz, a world-renowned specialist who was head of colorectal oncology at New York's Memorial Sloan-Kettering Cancer Center, along with his colleague Philip (Pat) Paty, a distinguished surgeon and researcher who specialized in complex cancers.

We quickly learned that in the U.S. the billing meter starts running the moment a patient sets foot in the lobby. Fortunately, BCG had a comprehensive private health insurance plan, and Tony had excellent connections, but even then David found it difficult to get all the talking time he wanted with the leading lights in cancer treatment. Whenever we saw Dr. Salz, he never took a seat during our visits, indicating we were not going to receive more than the allotted twenty minutes. This frustrated and rankled David, who wanted as much information and attention as he could squeeze out of every visit. Pat Paty, on the other hand, was very responsive, even giving up one Saturday to go through the results of a research project we had commissioned and to review different treatment options.

David also set about making healthy lifestyle changes. He found a Zen master and life coach named Philip, who — wouldn't you know? — was Jewish! He hired a yoga instructor to come to our house and take him through breathing, relaxation, and meditation exercises. Though David initiated these practices as part of his aggressive attack against cancer, he really did take to the spirit and knowledge of Eastern teachings. Since calming his overactive mind had always been a challenge, I was amazed to see him drift down from our third floor after a yoga session wearing an almost blissful look, and moving slowly, deliberately through the rest of his day.

David also took a keen interest in changing his diet. When I first met him, he loved every kind of food in great quantity — everything except beets. Back then, he was not a healthy eater. On Saturdays and Sundays, he would consume the same lunch his father had eaten for years in Sioux City — a hot dog loaded with everything, potato chips, and a side of cottage cheese, all washed down with a Coke. His breakfasts were healthier, but gargantuan, consisting of a mixing bowl with three types of cereal and as many kinds of fruit as we had in the house. In restaurants, he didn't want us to order the same dish because he always liked to "taste" mine, which was probably why I never gained weight while he packed on a few pounds.

After David's cancer returned, he came to see food as a frontline attack against his toxic invader. For breakfast, he added more protein to his big bowl of grains, topped with berries, berries, and more berries because of their cancer-fighting properties. He put turmeric on everything for the same reason. David's bibles for diet reform were two books coauthored by Richard Beliveau and Denis Gingras: *Foods That Fight Cancer* and *Cooking with Foods That Fight Cancer*. I grocery shopped every day and followed the cookbook's recipes in preparing his meals. Whenever we went to friends for dinner, David would take copies of these books along with the wine, eager as always to share his knowledge.

David also went through what I came to regard as his "heroic period," in which he had to be the life of every party, the epicentre of every exchange. David would dominate the room, sharing the excitement of his newest venture with an always appreciative audience. I would seat myself as inconspicuously and as far away as possible, withdrawing as his siblings used to when David was taking up all that conversational space at the family dinner table. As he became more frail physically, David became a stronger, more formidable presence.

David's medical research produced three lines of attack: chemotherapy, the most generalized; radiation, more focused; and surgery, the most targeted of all. Typically, he voted for a max attack: chemotherapy, followed by radiation and then surgery. I had attended all of David's appointments and had taken careful notes, which I had then checked against Tony's notes. Dr. Paty of Sloan-Kettering had told us that he had tracked about fifteen cases of David's rare syndrome, and that every patient had responded well to chemotherapy. I had also heard Dr. Salz tell David even more pointedly, "You will live or die by chemotherapy." Some of Dr. Salz's patients had survived twelve to sixteen years by changing the type of chemo when their bodies became resistant to the one they were using. In sum: David's cancer was systemic, meaning it was throughout his body. So was chemo as a treatment. Dr. Salz had advised, "If we can prolong your life for a decade, who knows what new cancer-fighting tools researchers may have developed?"

To undergo radiation, David would have to stop his chemo, and on top of that, the surgery would be difficult and risky. Though long-term chemo treatment was his best hope, David was as entrepreneurial in dealing with his cancer as he was with all other aspects of his life. Time and again, I would listen to David persuading our friends, along with himself and me, that chemo plus radiation plus surgery was the right choice. He was so convincing that even those with medical backgrounds would nod their heads and say, "That sounds plausible." David wanted to beat the odds, and we all hoped that he would. My heart was set on having him around for at least another ten years, maybe twenty if we got very lucky.

David began his chemotherapy treatments in Toronto in February 2007. His body was responsive, and tolerated chemo well. He was still working full-time for BCG. He was still attending meetings for DiverseCity and Greening Greater Toronto. No one seeing him would guess anything was wrong. Although he was pushing himself too hard, I supported the idea that he should live in the present, not dwell on fears for the future. We even attended the August 2008 Democratic convention in Denver, where Barack Obama was nominated as his party's presidential candidate. David had a knack for always knowing someone who could get us in anywhere. In this case, Ali Merali, a young friend who worked for Obama, opened doors for us. Since David was still an American citizen, he was able to make a donation, allowing us to attend events open to financial supporters — everything, in other words. We had the most amazing experience!

———————

David's radiation treatments began in February 2009, at Sloan-Kettering in New York. Radiation was his choice, and I didn't want to second-guess this decision any more than I already had. It's too easy and too heartbreaking to imagine where an untravelled road might have led.

David was to be on radiation for twenty-five days, with weekends off. Each session was only twenty minutes or so, and involved wearing a body suit with openings that targeted precisely the right areas to be zapped. After each morning's treatment, I had imagined we could hang out together in New York, one of our favourite cities, then have dinner somewhere and maybe go to a play. We did that on only one evening, with our friend Jennifer Wardrop, who happened to be in New York on business. Other than that, David was working so hard at his BCG New York office, fielding conference calls, even giving CBC radio interviews about one project or another, that I barely saw him. No one would have guessed that he was so ill. How could he possibly be sick when he was still everywhere, doing everything? As far as anyone outside our intimate circle was concerned, David was saving the world as usual with a full-service medical team at the ready.

After one particularly difficult visit with Dr. Salz, we went to lunch to process his bleak news. It was very hard to deal with the odds against us. David told me, "It's not that I'm afraid to die, but I have trouble imagining Sarah and Becca not having a father. Amy and Lauren will be okay, because they have two fathers, so they will still have one left."

That was a thought we hadn't allowed ourselves to express, but it hit us both very hard. I realized then that I was just beginning to say goodbye.

For March break 2009, Sarah and Becca joined friends of our family in a house they had rented for a week on Kiawah Island off the coast of South Carolina. It was something we often did as a family, with other families. David encouraged me to spend a few days with them, because he was busy with medical appointments and work in New York.

When I got back to New York, David had developed a deep, barking cough. He was sucking on Fisherman's Friend menthol lozenges — bags and bags of them — but the cough got worse and his voice grew hoarser. I had an awful premonition that something very bad had happened to him. Since he'd finished his radiation in April, we returned to Toronto. His surgery was scheduled for early July 2009, but I wondered if he would be too sick to have it. Sure enough, X-rays revealed foreign matter in his lungs, calling for follow-up MRIs.

On May 25, David and I hosted an engagement brunch for Lauren and her fiancé, Matt Lawrence, who were to be married in October. It was a beautiful sunny day, and our garden was festive with friends. Since David was so very hoarse, we had agreed that I would speak for both of us, while he might manage the toast.

Instead of raising his glass with a few token words, David started reminiscing about Great-Great-Grandfather Gustav. No one could imagine where he was going with this, or how he would circle back to the engaged couple, but somehow he managed to pull it all off. We were surprised and thrilled to have him back in storytelling mode.

It was a wonderful party, but we were worried about the appointment we had scheduled with Dr. Brezden-Masley at St. Mike's the next day. We would be receiving the results of the MRI, and we were bracing for bad news. The moment we saw Christine, our fears were confirmed. She said, "I'm sorry …" and showed us David's X-rays. He had masses of what she termed "ground glass" in his lungs. As the MRI tests had confirmed, they were permeated with cancer.

David looked so stunned that Christine spontaneously hugged him. Then she hugged me. I knew she was telling us it was only a matter of time.

David said, "My daughter's getting married in October."

Christine replied, "Ask her to move up the wedding."

David looked even more disoriented. As someone who didn't believe in defeat, he couldn't grasp that this was happening.

It was a struggle for David to get his fighting spirit back, but he managed it. He continued his aggressive chemo treatments. He assembled a bigger BCG research team. Though his breathing was ever more laboured and he was on oxygen around the clock, he still insisted on going to the office for meetings. He wanted to keep moving, not only to distract himself but also because he had always turned his work into an adventure that rewarded his enthusiasm. The same was true of his volunteer projects. One of his great frustrations was that his life had been interrupted at precisely the point when he felt at the height of his powers. A pro bono project that used to take him a month to convene, he now had the credentials and the connections and the knowhow to set up in an hour. Having ratcheted his talents to this new level, he no longer even had to do much to prime the pump. Participants' expectations ran so high that as soon as he had them in the same room, ideas would start to flow with an attack plan to follow.

Early in July 2009, our daughter, Sarah, was due to return to Camp Wapomeo in Algonquin Park for another epic canoe trip. David, Sarah, and I drove up north and stayed overnight at Deerhurst Inn before leaving the campers at dockside the next day. David hadn't been feeling well, and by the time we reached Huntsville on our way home, he seemed feverish. We called Christine, and she told us to go straight to St. Mike's emergency.

As a downtown hospital that handled more than its share of shootings and muggings, St. Mike's emergency department is not a great place to be on a weekend. We had a long wait before David was put into isolation because of the threat of H1N1, and without anyone having done much for him. The next day, at his request, I brought him home, where he fell into bed, exhausted. Then he became so sick, with so much trouble breathing, that I drove him back to St. Mike's. When the girls and I visited, we had to dress in protective caps and gowns and gloves, like figures from outer space, so as not to compromise his weakened immune system with outside contamination.

Because David was in semi-isolation, only family and close friends could visit. Lauren had flown in from California to spend time with him and to share plans for her wedding in Malibu on October 10. Remembering Christine's warning about moving up the date, David suggested that he might not last that long. With calm conviction, Lauren replied, "It's ninety-nine days until then, David, and I know you'll be there to walk me down the aisle." Her confidence was infectious. The wedding plans didn't change.

David found being in the hospital unbearable and again pleaded with me, "Get me out! I'm never going to get well here."

I worked hard to gain his discharge, and finally succeeded. Lauren and I were sitting by his bed, no longer in caps and gowns, when a nurse arrived.

She demanded, "Where is your sterile gear?"

I replied, "But my husband is going home now."

She closed the door. "Oh no he's not! We just got his test results. He has H1N1."

I was astonished. "What? He's been here a week, and you're just finding that out now?"

She replied, "He's probably over the worst of it."

And he was. Here was this guy, rife with cancer, on a breathing apparatus, so sick from H1N1 that it could have killed a healthy person, but he had willed himself to survive. That was David. His incredible resilience. His unquenchable desire to live. His determination to be a one-percenter.

Our family even managed a vacation early in August — to Martha's Vineyard, an island off the coast of Cape Cod in Massachusetts. We flew down by chartered jet to make it as easy as possible for David. Unfortunately, David's luggage fell off the cart when it was being transported to the tiny terminal and was dragged a hundred yards by a passing vehicle. The bag was destroyed, with most of its contents charred or lost. David calmly remarked that he was lucky that the important things had survived: his Luminato hat, his books, one pair of socks, and some underwear.

David had a good time despite his oxygen tank. We even have a picture of him attempting to slide down a banister. For his last swim, I have another picture of him in the swimming pool floating on an inflatable beaver. He was smiling.

Another member of the Pecaut family died that summer. On August 19, David's father, Dick, age seventy-eight, passed away. This was no surprise. He had been diagnosed with what was thought to be pancreatic cancer. The autopsy would reveal that it was melanoma, one of the deadliest of cancers because it can travel anywhere. Years before, he'd had a growth on one leg removed, and now the cancer had spread to his stomach. Only three weeks passed between diagnosis and death.

Dick had remarried a year after Dottie had died in 1997, which was exactly what Dottie had wanted for him because she felt he was not the sort of person who should live alone. Just before her own passing, Dottie had shared with David an approved list of potential mates for Dick. Months later, when Dick told David he was seeing a woman named Marilyn, David had good reason to hope that she was on the list, since it contained two Marilyns. Sure enough, Marilyn Moody had been a high school pal of Dottie's whose husband had died of cancer the year before. Marilyn and Dick were a good match. Marilyn laughed even harder than Dick at all his old jokes because, as she explained, "I just love the way he tells them!"

A few years before Dottie's death, Dick had collapsed while playing tennis. This ultimately led to a diagnosis of multiple sclerosis. Being a Pecaut, Dick fought back vigorously. Though he had to give up his favourite activities, tennis and golf, he managed to walk two miles every day until his legs weakened and even standing became difficult. Dick also searched relentlessly for treatments. One homeopathic remedy, enjoying a modicum of success, was bee venom, deposited by stinging. Dick went so far as to purchase his own bee colony before deciding the treatment was of limited value to him.

Since MS doesn't kill most of its victims, Dick sometimes wondered what would be his nemesis. After more than a decade of managing MS without complaint, he may have been relieved to know he would soon be giving up his daily struggle. On learning he had terminal cancer, he requested, "No chemo, no radiation, not even a biopsy. Just keep me comfortable." For this, he chose St. Luke's Hospital, where he had served on the board; where his daughter, Stacey, was a chaplain; where Marilyn could stay in the room and sleep on a cot by his side; and where it was convenient for friends, family, and colleagues to visit.

David often spoke publicly about the strong influence his mother had in shaping his interest in community and family. But he also recognized that his father was a different and equally powerful force in his life. In a letter he wrote to his dad a month before Dick died, David was anticipating his own death and drawing some parallels: "I know facing my own cancer this past year that I draw on the strength that you and Mom showed me. We cannot choose our challenges, but we can choose how we face them. And you have always faced yours head-on with strength and courage."

David believed that the greatest gift his father had given him was the confidence to make his own decisions. "I remember that when I was about twelve years old and had my paper route money that I wanted to invest, you invited me to your office and sat me in front of five company annual reports," he wrote. "You said I should read about them and then choose one. I chose Brunswick Corporation because it made bowling equipment and all the kids I knew were crazy for bowling. Also they had medical equipment, and I knew that as people were growing older that would be a growth market. But the important thing was you let me choose. You wanted me to feel confident I could make that kind of decision — and many others." David instilled that same sense of confidence in his own children when it came to making choices.

Dick's funeral took place on August 29 at St. Thomas' Episcopal Church, where he had served on the vestry and spearheaded its building restoration program. Our four daughters were among Dick's thirteen grandchildren who served as pallbearers. David was not only present but also managed to speak. When it was Dan's turn, he compared Dick Pecaut's last days, during which the whole neighbourhood paid tribute, to the *what if* requiem for Jimmy Stewart's character in *It's A Wonderful Life*.

David believed his father had chosen to die before him, his oldest son, because he couldn't bear to subvert the natural order.

CHAPTER SIXTEEN

A Wedding and a Funeral

I t was a gorgeous day toward the end of September 2009 when David and I went to Mount Pleasant to choose a burial site.

We had just had our last lunch together at Tabule on Yonge Street. Well, I had lunch. David's mouth was so blistered and raw from the chemo that he found even the mildest Middle Eastern dishes too spicy. It was there that I broached the sensitive subject, "Would you like to go to the cemetery with me?" I presented it as the search for a *family* plot. "It's where you and I will be buried together some day."

We picked out a site the same way as we had selected our home. I was to scout for options, then bring in David for the final decision. Again, he had instructions for me. He didn't want to be in some out-of-the-way place where people would have to search for him. He didn't want to be too prominent, but he did want to be evident. "And I'd like a bench where the kids can sit and talk to me."

It was so strange, looking at real estate again, but for such a poignant purpose, and with David burdened by his breathing tank. As with our house, I showed him three potential places, leaving what I knew to be the best until last. He declared the first location too crowded, like a suburb where the houses are all crammed together. The second spot was on a corner, which he found too open and exposed. Then I showed him the third option, the one I favoured. "It faces south, and points almost straight to our house."

David thought about it for a minute and replied, "Yes, this feels right."

"It's where I'd also like to be one day. We can put a bench here for the kids when they come to visit." My voice broke, and so did my heart as I was saying this. But like so many other sad tasks, it had to be done and I wanted to make the decision with David.

Lauren's wedding to Matt Lawrence was scheduled for October 10 in Malibu. While David was in the hospital, she had kept saying to him, "It's only ninety-nine days to the wedding. You'll be there ... It's only ninety-eight days to the wedding. You'll be there."

Lauren just wouldn't give in. Of course, she wanted to keep her wedding as she'd planned it, but she also had complete confidence that David would make it to October to walk her down the aisle.

She was right. Lauren had two fathers that day. Ron, her dad, was on her left, while David, her step-dad, was on her right.

Getting David ready was quite a production. Since I was with the female half of the bridal party, participating in the ritual of having hair and nails done, David asked his oldest friend, Rich Levy, to dress him. Helping him into his tuxedo and cummerbund was as arduous as armouring a knight for battle. David had to keep sitting down to catch his breath, but Rich felt honoured to have been asked, and patiently, devotedly prepared his friend for the occasion.

The wedding was outdoors on a bluff overlooking the Pacific Ocean, and it was a very long aisle leading to the altar. Many people cried to see Lauren so lovingly flanked by her two fathers. Though David was almost permanently attached to his oxygen tank, he had left it behind in the car, determined to breathe unassisted. He looked so happy and proud and normal that you would never know anything was wrong.

David also attended the reception. Though he couldn't speak, Ron acknowledged him with great charm and generosity, and David was so excited to be surrounded by family and friends, many of whom had come for him as much as for the bride. Any extra exertion, including dancing, was difficult, but that didn't stop him from stepping out on the floor with Lauren to fulfill his father-of-the-bride role. The rest of the time he stayed on the sidelines, but he was there. Dan said he'd never seen his brother so joyful. It was as if David's impending death had allowed him to dig even deeper into his appreciation for life.

Before Lauren and Matt's wedding, David had been coming downstairs each morning for breakfast, then returning to our bedroom at the end of each day. Though we had portable oxygen tanks everywhere, he was so afraid of running out that I stocked our main floor with huge containers from an oxygen supply company so that our dining room looked like a brewery. The sign on our front door warned: no matches, no candles, and certainly no smoking.

It was only very occasionally, and for very special reasons, that David left our house. Toward the end of October, he and Tony Gagliano had a meeting with Premier Dalton McGuinty to provide an update on Luminato.

David dressed very slowly that morning, then made his way downstairs with frequent stops. I helped him into the car and drove him to Queen's Park.

David asked, "Is there an entrance where I won't have to climb stairs?"

Having worked at the legislature for many years, I knew the building inside and out. "Yes, I know just the place where you can walk straight in."

I parked as near as possible, then asked, "Should I go with you?"

"No, please. I want to walk by myself."

"I'll wait here for you."

"No. I'll get a taxi."

I watched as David walked slowly to the entrance of the legislature, wheeling his oxygen tank. As soon as he came in view of others, he composed himself and, with a feat of will, quickened his pace. He was remarkable!

Describing the meeting, the premier said, "My office had learned years ago that if Mr. Pecaut wanted a meeting, resistance was futile. So, there sat David, accompanied by his Luminato co-conspirator, Tony. David's face was drawn. His hair was thin. His movements, laboured. His breathing, aided by the oxygen canister he had in tow. David had come in to see me to make sure I understood just how important Luminato was to Toronto. I sat there and I marvelled at the man. His endurance. His persistence. But above all, his selflessness."

He remembered, "In times past, David would walk into our meetings with a big bundle of meticulous notes. Or with an innocent-looking slide deck. He had a disarming grin and an easy charm, which he used to his advantage. David never played fair. And I never had a chance. Because his ideas were always solid and exciting. His enthusiasm, infectious. And his cause, most worthy. In short, he was an irresistible force."

After the wedding, David began having more difficulty navigating the stairs, so he elected to stay on the second floor, taking his meals and receiving visitors there. I rented a special hospital bed, and the girls and I would eat upstairs in my office next door at a folding dining table supplied by our friends, Lisa Olfman and David Wolfe. He also used this as a conference table where he could work on matters he felt needed his attention or those that continued to hold his enthusiasm. This was also where he had his official last visits with a number of people who had been very important to him. It was here he had his last conversation with his Harvard friend and partner in the Boreal Institute, Jamie Radner, and where he said goodbye to his mentor and role model, Dr. John Evans.

When David found even walking from one room to the next difficult, we settled him fully into the bedroom, where he alternated between the bed and the chair. Eventually, his lungs became so compromised, his breathing so laboured, and his energy so low that he gave in to the inevitable and stayed in bed.

During the last eight weeks of David's life, he received excellent nursing care from a team from St. Elizabeth Home Care. Dr. Russell Goldman, a palliative care specialist from the Temi Latner Centre, took particular interest in him, visited frequently, and offered thoughtful answers to his often difficult questions.

The more David felt the loss of his body, the harder he worked to control everything he could control. He wanted to know what nurse would be coming and when, so he made a little chart for himself. He kept meticulous records as to what pills he should be taking each day and when: 9:20 a.m., 12:40, 2:00 … His last entry was on Saturday, November 21, and then he couldn't write anymore.

David liked to give everyone a special task. Our neighbour and friend James Deacon supplied the notepads on which David scribbled messages to spare his fading voice. Only James was allowed to do that. Jennifer Wardrop, another close friend, was assigned to grind the onions that produced the fumes David used to help clear his nasal passages, and only Jennifer was allowed to do that. My cousin Rick Fox, an ear, throat, and nose specialist, was on call to clear David's breathing passages when they became too congested for onion fumes. Bob Casper, another friend and also a doctor (albeit a gynecologist!), supplied from his fertility clinic the sterile funnels that David insisted he needed for a special humidifier that he used only twice.

Then there was the quest for the perfect pillow. Since David found it difficult to get comfortable, Kathy Elder, another friend, was dispatched to find a better one. She came back with a dozen, all shapes and sizes, some stuffed with down and others with microfibre. Afterwards, when I came into David's bedroom, he was sitting propped in bed with a sweet smile on his face. My pillow was missing from its usual place in our bed. He had wrapped it around his neck. From then on, no other would do.

Even when family and friends flew in to say their goodbyes, David set them to work. Jonathan Guss and Leslie Milrod spent five hours at David's bedside one afternoon as he dictated a series of instructions for how to help Becca get into Harvard or any top U.S. college of her choice. Jonathan later captured that wisdom in a thirty-two-page manual that demonstrates David's determination to help his kids succeed.

If a family photo or a BCG file was on one side of the room, David would invariably want it moved to the other side. When Dan came to visit, he had expected to hang out with his brother, perhaps reminisce over shared memories. Wasn't that what he had learned at his dying mother's bedside? Just *to be*. What Dan learned at his brother's bedside was that *to be* was *not to be*. David had him hauling away so many books that I had to install new shelves in the playroom to accommodate them.

Dan had also been selected to put David's financial affairs in order. "David's mind was going a thousand miles a minute with BCG conference calls and colleagues and friends and college buddies wanting to see him. It was heady stuff, very intense, like visiting a head of state with everyone, including me, being slotted into what Helen called 'a good window,'" he later recalled. "It was almost comical. Here was David, on oxygen, essentially bedridden, and I was the worn-out one saying, 'Why don't you take a nap?' while he was insisting, 'No, no, we have to get all this wrapped up today.' It was just like when we were kids. My big brother was the field general."

David had always handled much of our investing, while I looked after the more mundane family finances, such as paying the bills. It was now necessary for me to be briefed fully on where our money was and what the investment strategy was. Though I possess a good business mind and have handled money very competently, David chose to explain everything to Dan, to our accountant, and to our estate lawyer, with me as a listener. I remember one conversation with Dan, David, and myself around our sunroom table. David had managed to come downstairs, but his lack of oxygen and all his medications were affecting his clarity so that he was explaining everything to us for the nth time. Dan was nodding and I was nodding, when David suddenly demanded, "Do you understand what I'm talking about?"

I started to cry for only the second time since his worst diagnosis. I said, "I *do* understand. I just don't want you to go."

David didn't cry. He just steeled himself. Perhaps he feared that his despair, unleashed, would kill him sooner.

When it was time for Dan to say his last goodbye, the brothers kissed, while Dan's airport limousine idled at curbside.

As Dan headed for the door, David called out, "Wait! One more kiss."

Dan returned, then started to leave again.

"Wait, come back!"

The brothers shared another kiss, the way two innocent young boys used to throw kisses to each other, each night, before nodding off to sleep.

No one wanted to live more than David, but underneath all his optimism, he could see what the future would be like without his physical presence. He knew he would never be walking Amy or Sarah or Becca down the aisle, but he still wanted, somehow, to be a part of their lives. Lauren was charged with purchasing four copies each of the favourite books we read to the kids when they were young, including *The Little Engine That Could*, *Are You My Mother?*, *I'll Love You Forever*, and *The Giving Tree*. There were also the four children's books our family always read at Christmas: *Peef the Christmas Bear, The Night Before Christmas, Eloise at Christmastime,* and *How the Grinch Stole Christmas.* David inscribed each book to his future grandchildren: "Dearest ... How I'd love to be reading this to you with you sitting on my lap." He signed them, "Papa David."

David wrote a letter to his BCG colleagues, expressing his joy in working with them and his gratitude for their support throughout his illness. Most importantly, David wrote letters to our daughters, expressing his special pride in each one, to be read on the morning of their first Christmas without him — two weeks and one day after his passing.

David also entrusted to me the writing of this memoir, for which he'd left copious notes, three days of audiotaped interviews with our friend David Wolfe, plus many hours of videotaped interviews with BCG "historian" Ted Buswick, videographer Bob Pomerantz, and our daughter Becca. David's assistant Lucy Bellisario had carefully assembled and organized the written and digital archives capturing David's speeches, notes, and presentations over his thirty-year career. There was no shortage of material to work with.

David hesitated at first to ask me about taking on the role of his biographer. No one had had as many encounters with all the voices of David as I, but since we were totally honest with one another, he might have thought I knew him too well and would not present him as valiantly as he hoped. Or maybe he just didn't want to burden me with yet another writing assignment, one that would be so emotionally taxing.

In the end, we both acknowledged I was the only person who could capture David's story. I agreed to do it, in my own way, but not right away. Then David made us laugh by proving how well *he* knew *me*: "Don't wait too long or you'll get too busy with other things."

Like Dan, I would have preferred to have more time with David just *to be* rather than *to do.* Many people I scarcely knew felt a sense of entitlement around him, and took private time from our family. As an excuse to leave the house, I ran errands or went shopping for a couple of hours every day. I never bought anything. I just wandered around aimlessly, looking at pretty things. I was still surrounded by people, but I didn't have to do anything, I didn't have to say anything, and I didn't have to explain what I was doing. I was shopping.

Though David didn't talk much anymore, he continued to write notes, some of which were hilarious. When our friend Tracey Sobers came to visit, he flashed one to her that caused her to burst out laughing. It said, "Isn't Helen hot?" I found it very reassuring that the David I knew was still in the same room with me, despite his frailty.

I planned David's funeral in consultation with him. He was engaged, but he no longer had any strong feelings. He was trying to conserve his strength to live as long as possible.

Since David said he didn't want anything religious, I left one suggestion to the very end, ready to withdraw it at his slightest hesitation: "I've been thinking ... our family is so unusual in that we have three major world religions in one generation: Christianity, Judaism, and Islam. What if Uncle George, my brother, and I do the Mourner's Kaddish, and Dan and your sisters say a Christian prayer, and Youssouf and his girls read verses from the Qur'an?"

Though David had been silent and still for days, he turned to me and whispered, "I think it's brilliant."

On the morning of December 14, which was a Monday, David was unable to communicate in any way. The sterile funnel he used to get air had to be put over his whole face, and when the nurse removed it he couldn't even open his eyes. He seemed to be aware, but he had no energy and barely any breath.

Our friend, Martin Knelman, the *Toronto Star* arts columnist, had phoned for biographical material and to check the accuracy of a quote, obviously for David's obituary. It was after eight. The night nurse had left, and Elizabeth, the morning nurse, was due to arrive any minute. I hadn't had my breakfast, and I was still in my robe and slippers when I went into my office to get the information for Martin.

Elizabeth came in. "He's gone," she said.

My hands froze above my computer keyboard. Despite all the anticipation of this moment, I couldn't believe it had happened. I ran into our bedroom and stared at David. "How do you know?" I asked.

She replied, "There's no pulse."

I exclaimed, "He's never alone. How could it happen when no one was here?"

Elizabeth replied, "People often choose to go when no one is with them. They know it's their time, and they take their leave."

I protested, "It's so sad that David was alone!"

"No, he waited until you weren't at his side because he didn't want you to see him leave. He knew you were right next door. He died in a house full of his loved ones."

She was right. All of us were home except for Lauren, who had been here for a few days during which she'd scarcely left David's bedside.

How had David managed to find that one moment when he was alone? That's still beyond me.

First, I went to the girls, huddled together on Becca's bed, to talk and to cry. I had no idea what to do next, so I called my friend Linda to ask her advice on how to make the necessary arrangements. After I had made all those practical calls, I returned to the bedroom. Linda was sitting there with David! I had no recollection of asking her to come over, and no idea how she could have arrived so quickly. She reminded me of the Jewish tradition of never leaving a body unattended. Someone must be present to assure a safe passage to heaven, so there she was.

When David was taken from our house, I made sure the girls were not present. I didn't want that to be their last view of their father.

CHAPTER SEVENTEEN

Remembering David

A light snow was falling on the morning of December 21, 2009, the day of David's memorial service. Our family was driven the short distance to Rosedale United Church by limo and escorted discreetly into the rear entrance of the building, avoiding the crowd that had gathered outside.

Someone asked me later why I had chosen such a "small venue" for the service, which was attended by over five hundred people. David and I had agreed on Rosedale United Church, where our kids had performed in school concerts, with minister Karen Bowles, a neighbour and friend, officiating. The children would be asked to speak, along with David's brother and sisters. Then there would be John Paul MacDuffie and Lloyd David from Harvard, Rich Levy from Sioux City, and John Clarkeson from BCG. Tony Gagliano was a natural choice, as was Premier Dalton McGuinty and John Evans, who had been a mentor and like a second father to David. For music, I invited Dan and his very talented children to sing a cappella, as they had so beautifully and so recently at Dick's memorial service. John Paul supplied CDs for musical interludes, a selection that included Bill Evans's *My Foolish Heart* and Chopin's *Nocturnes*.

Many remarked on how "uplifting" the service was and how much laughter filled the room as each speaker offered warm, funny stories about David. Many were anecdotes that no one, including myself, had ever heard. Sadly, this confirmed what David and I often said after attending a funeral service: you never really know someone until that person moves into the past tense.

Becca and Amy rose to the podium first and spoke on behalf of all four daughters. There was a titter in the room as Becca recalled her dad's determination to ensure Gustav's place in our family history. "In fact, I was almost named Gus, after Great-Great-Grandfather Gustav Pecaut, who worked his way into so many of Dad's stories and speeches." Good thing she was a girl!

Amy recalled that David never ran out of material to entertain their friends and that "if it weren't for my mom and all of us girls, he would still be wearing a green polyester suit and carrying his files around in plastic shopping bags." What she added was a little more poignant and not as well known. "Though he was proud of what he achieved and how he changed so many people's lives, he told us he would have given up all these successes just to have a little more time with his girls."

David's brother Dan marvelled at two special gifts that he received from David. One was the ability to keep your inner child alive, which he saw as "the taproot of David's effusive personality." The other gift was the unique way David thought. Dan referred to German mathematician Carl Jacobi, who exhorted his students to "Invert, always invert!" And that's what David did instinctively. "While many of us try to think outside the box, David *lived* outside the box."

"David Kent Pecaut. His name tells his story," said his sister, Shelley. The Pecaut side of the family represented adventure, a pioneer spirit, an acumen for business, and deep roots in the American Midwest. "But David was also a Kent, and though the story was heard less frequently, David was equally proud of this DNA set. The Kents were a family of champions: John Kent won the World Three Legged Race, and his global success inspired David to run cross-country track in high school."

David's college roommates, John Paul and Lloyd, spoke of David as "someone whose ambition was exceeded only by his optimism, and whose urge to fly was only partly impeded by such earthly matters as gravity."

Rich Levy described the Boy Scout, cross-country runner, and decent church-league basketball player who was full of bad jokes and could have emerged from a Norman Rockwell painting. "It was hard not to love him."

John Clarkeson recalled that David was a natural at consulting, one of only a handful he had ever met. "He had a ninety-ninth percentile ability to go from complete ignorance to world-class expert in less time than you and I could click on Google." Anticipating how much David's colleagues would miss his ideas, his energy, and his enthusiasm, the BCG team in Toronto were already asking themselves: "What would David do? What would he see that we're missing?" They're still asking.

John Evans noted that David's intellectual prowess was matched by an EQ that was "off the chart." David's network was so extensive that "apparently his Rolodex included over a thousand names on the active file and his BlackBerry required RIM to install additional memory."

Dalton McGuinty described the last time he and his wife, Terri, visited to say goodbye. Too weak to rise from the chair or even lift a book, David asked Dalton to pull down from the shelf his three-volume set on the life of Lyndon Johnson. "Observing my intimidation at the size of my reading assignment — these are massive volumes — David said: 'Now, Dalton, don't worry about reading the whole thing. Just read the first volume. I think you'll find it helpful in your work.'"

Tony Gagliano spoke about his big brother — "not one that was given to me at birth but one that was chosen by my heart." He described David as an impatient optimist who knew Toronto was getting better, but it was not getting better fast enough and it was not getting better for everyone. Tony imagined David already having his face-to-face meeting with God and collaborating with arts leaders who have gone before us to create a heavenly version of Luminato, "and it will no doubt be more ambitious than our earthly festival."

There were hundreds of letters and emails following David's death — so many that it was all I could do to read them, let alone respond. One of those letters was from our friend Jonathan Guss, who noted, "David was at the centre of an incredibly complex Venn diagram which he called the Toronto Region's civil society. His indomitable enthusiasm was infectious and drove large groups of sophisticated people to achieve dreams that gray-haired Conventional Wisdom had declared impossible. We all assumed that that energy was an infinitely renewable resource. Alas, life is life."

———————

In September 2009, three months before David's death, he had sent a fascinating email to our friend Atom Egoyan: "One of the funny things about my situation is how I wake up. Most mornings I wake up very happy and feeling good. As I gradually gain consciousness, I begin to become aware of my situation and the illness and how much things have changed."

David's transition from a blissful sense that everything was right with his world to the brutal reality that it was not came as a surprise each day. He went on to speculate, "There is always this strange sense of why I wake in a state from the past. And why I have forgotten. Perhaps we always wake like this, but we go through it too quickly and so miss the forgetting part and sense of the past."

David's email, ending "It seems like a cinematic experience," was the spur for Atom to curate the transformation of this highly personal experience into a work of art to be shared with the world. The result was a two-part installation, unveiled as the opening event for Luminato 2010. *Solar Breath* by Michael Snow was a sixty-two-minute loop of fluttering curtains across a window that overlooks a sunny yard. *Light Air*, a response to Snow's work, was by Mani Mazinani, a young Toronto artist. Fittingly, this installation was in Brookfield Place, where BCG has its Toronto office. It allowed the spirit of David to become a continuing part of Luminato, the festival he loved so much, in celebration of the city he loved with equal devotion.

There were other public tributes for David — an outpouring that seemed to fill the media, and was sometimes overwhelming to the girls and to me. David had become something of a local hero. Everyone wrote about his or her experience of him, and we realized how deeply and widely our grief was shared.

To my surprise, I found I needed a shiva for David, something more personal and private than the memorial service and the visitation that was attended by hundreds of mourners on the Sunday evening before it. I called on my closest friends, Lisa and Linda, to help me plan an impromptu shiva — two days of open-door visits to our home.

David's sister Shelley, her husband, Youssouf, and their children stayed with us over Christmas. Our family read aloud the four books we always had, then distributed the books David had inscribed for his unborn grandchildren. When our girls opened the letters David had so lovingly dictated and signed for each of them, I realized that there wasn't one for me. I think he just ran out of time.

After Christmas, our family and some friends flew to La Jolla on the California coast — a place where we had vacationed a few years ago with David and his family to celebrate Dick's seventieth birthday. We stayed at the same grand hotel, La Valencia, filled with the fondest of memories. Lauren and Matt joined us from Los Angeles, having driven down in David's old Lexus. Being the lone male among eight women gave Matt a sense of "being David," as we often joked that week.

We returned to our home with some trepidation. How would it feel without David? He had made me promise not to sell the house for at least ten years because he wanted the children to continue to have a family home. "I'll always be there," he had assured me.

I'm a strong believer in reincarnation. David thought this odd, because he saw me as a pragmatist, but reincarnation makes sense to me. We don't just disappear, we turn into something else. With David's embrace of Buddhism, the idea of continuity made sense to him as well. One day I heard him tell the girls, "You know that if you need me, I'll be on your shoulder, so you'll be able to turn and find me there." Another time, he told Sarah, "I'll come back as a butterfly, or something else that you'll recognize." Everywhere we go, and especially at significant moments, butterflies circle and then land on Sarah. It happens when we are sitting on our back deck. It happens at Dairymen's, the Pecaut family's Wisconsin retreat, where we continue to vacation. When a butterfly lands, Sarah and I look at each other silently but knowingly, not wanting to spoil the magic.

David keeps coming back to each of us in other ways. Last summer, after Amy decided to start her own public relations business, she found a note from David, anticipating this venture. He asked her to celebrate at a special dinner with the whole family, to make sure we had champagne, and to include him in the toast.

Only a couple of weeks before David died, he urged a newly married Lauren to have children as soon as possible. Though she and Matt had planned to wait a while, somehow she managed to get pregnant while still on birth control. Their daughter — our granddaughter, Paityn Davy Lawrence — was born on October 4, 2010.

And then there's Becca, who wears David's sweaters, who shares his encyclopedic memory and his love of storytelling, and who looks, acts, and sounds like him in so many ways that it's uncanny. Though she's attending Gallatin School at NYU instead of Harvard, as she and her dad once planned, she knows her life will always reflect her father's hopes for her, including making her own decisions.

––––––––––

David remains very much a part of our ongoing lives. His office remains unchanged, with his family photos, his books about Toronto and Sioux City, his Haida masks, his name burned in wood as a gift from Amy, his three-volume Harvard thesis on community organization through weak ties, his Sussex M.A. thesis on music and philosophy, his file of exotic family vacations that we never had a chance to take. Mostly I feel David's presence when I am sitting on our back deck, his favourite place in the world, looking out on the garden that he loved so well, with the flowering trees planted for each of our daughters. We had such wonderful conversations on our back deck; we often had family dinners there, and we frequently welcomed friends there.

A friend whose husband had died a few months before David told me that one way to free a house of spirits was to freeze everything in it, including the marital bed. After her husband's passing, she had kept all her windows open for two days in the dead of winter to help her loved one's spirit travel into the next life. Though I was fascinated by her account and respected her advice, I told her, "But I don't want David to leave. I'm happy with him here."

Like his mother, David never wished anything to be named for him while he was alive. About two months after his death, I heard that an effort was underway to rename a public space for David. I was still feeling overwhelmed by loss. I also took to heart a piece of sound advice from a friend who had practised estate law, which is not to make any decisions or commitments in the first year. So I signalled to the well-intentioned people who wanted to name things after David that I wasn't prepared to entertain such a possibility yet. Then, in the fall of 2010, after Toronto had elected Rob Ford as its new mayor, his arts advisor, Jeff Melanson, met with Tony Gagliano and myself one evening at the Four Seasons Hotel to discuss naming a public space for David. Matters moved quickly for a while, went silent over Christmas, then picked up early in the new year.

As events were unfolding, I received a call from my local councillor. She said that she didn't know David, but that she understood that the family would be open to a public space being named after him.

She continued, "I've been looking at some possibilities and I understand that you live near Rosedale Subway? There's a parkette at the end of the street. Would that be of interest?"

My heart sank. The parkette was an unimpressive smidgen of grass dominated by bus and subway traffic. "It really doesn't speak to me of David," I replied, trying to be diplomatic.

We had a brief conversation about process before she added, almost as an afterthought, "Well … there's Metro Square."

Now my heart leapt. I quickly replied, "That would be fine."

"Of course, this would have to be approved by city council."

Our kids knew Dundas Square because they'd attended Luminato events there, but they didn't know Metro Square. They had their first glimpse as we emerged from the underground parking garage into its beautiful open spaces alive with people, its parks and benches and water sculptures reflected in glass towers.

"Wow! This is for Dad? It's huge!"

Now they were as thrilled and proud as I was, especially since I had learned that David Pecaut Square was to become the new outdoor hub for Luminato, to be filled with song and dance and celebration for ten glorious days every June.

A colleague at Queen's Park had been going through some difficult negotiations with City Hall and asked how on earth I managed to get them to rename Metro Square after David. "Easy," I replied. "They offered and I accepted." In fact, the mayor and his office couldn't have been more gracious and generous. All the more remarkable since Rob Ford told me at the official opening of the square that he had never met David, "but what he did for Toronto deserves to be remembered."

I remain close with David's colleagues at BCG, who are like family to me. When David was an ambitious young man, he absorbed everything he could from his partners with more experience. After he matured, he declared mentoring to be the greatest of all gifts, and he was eager to play that gift forward by coaching younger colleagues, by providing wise counsel to friends faced with problems he knew how to resolve, by encouraging the bright young people he encountered during his pro bono work.

It was these qualities in David that inspired the Pecaut Centre for Social Impact, a new venture that bears his name and continues his legacy. Its mission is to magnify social impact by convening people, knowledge, resources, and mentorship in support of Canada's next generation of promising social entrepreneurs, who will be called Pecaut Fellows. The Centre's venture philanthropy fund will also provide financial and other support to proven enterprises that can deliver a high social return on investment, with the intention of taking them to the national level, following the Pathways to Education trajectory of growth.

As founders, we kept asking ourselves while the concept was evolving, *What would David do?* As though anticipating that question, David had written in an article that appeared in *The Globe and Mail* in November 2007: "Canadian leaders are realizing that this new model of social entrepreneurship is uniquely suited to bring innovation to some of our most challenging social issues. Let's try some new models to attack old problems." Though it's early days for the Pecaut Centre, it is well on its way to becoming the new model that David envisaged.

David's many other projects carry on. Most of the boards and councils and projects that David helped to create still provide value for Toronto, Ontario and Canada. The Toronto City Summit Alliance has been re-branded CivicAction, a name David helped choose. Its programs are thriving, and the Summit of February 2011 attracted a large and engaged group of city builders who identified many important challenges yet to be tackled.

Luminato continues to reflect the dreams that David and Tony Gagliano shared. I am now on the Luminato board, and last year Sarah was an intern. Since David didn't want a tribute dinner or a prize named for him, each year there will be a new artistic tribute to David at Luminato. In 2010, it was the Snow/Mazinani collaboration, representing David's recurring dream. In 2011, it was the coffee table book *Luminato: Painting the Canvas of the City* with text by David Macfarlane and photographs by Nigel Dickson. In 2012, the Luminato hub at David Pecaut Square was defined and transformed by the winning design of architectural firm Diamond Schmitt. Next year and every year, there will be another design competition for the creative interpretation of this public space.

After the Luminato book was launched on June 9, guests moved seamlessly from the neighbouring Shore Club to the newly renamed square. A number of us spoke at the rededication that night — Tony Gagliano introduced me, I introduced the premier, and then David's brother Dan. Premier McGuinty expressed what many of us were feeling: how perfect this people place, surrounded by centres of art and culture, sports, finance, and municipal government, was for David, allowing him to continue to provide a forum for Torontonians to gather.

The premier also referred to the presence in the crowd of my Uncle George Fox, age ninety-four, noting that Uncle George had just bought a new car with an extended warranty and upgraded his treadmill to a faster model. Our family was delighted, since this was exactly the way David would have invoked Great-Great-Grandfather Gustav!

I remembered all the times I'd been asked, *What would David want?* Exactly this.

Last April, our family held our Easter egg hunt as usual, then took some of the decorated eggs to David's grave. I confess that I don't visit the cemetery very often. It's too sad. When I want to remember David — full of optimism and generosity and joy — I go to David Pecaut Square, and I sit on one of those benches, listening to its animated crowds at play, encircled by the richness of David's beloved Toronto.

The girls have caught some of this same spirit. One day, Amy announced, "You know, I think I'd like to get married in David Pecaut Square." When that wedding takes place in the spring of 2013, David will be there.

CHAPTER EIGHTEEN

The Last Chapter

I n the final weeks of David's life, he composed a letter that was published in the *Toronto Star* shortly before he died. Since crafting this important document at such an advanced stage in his illness was a difficult task for him, both physically and mentally, much of it was dictated to and edited by me — all twenty-plus versions. Known as David's "love letter to Toronto," it was a thank you, a rallying cry, and a goodbye. Being David, he wanted to write the last chapter of his life himself and instruct us in how to face the future together.

The last chapter of this book belongs to David.

———————

Friends and Colleagues,

As many of you know, I have been battling cancer over the past while and have been focusing in recent weeks on spending time with my family. I am truly lucky to be blessed with an incredible wife and children.

As a consequence of my health issues, I have not had the chance to see many of you and express my appreciation for all the work we have done together. Nor have I had the chance to share some of my thoughts on Toronto's future. This note gives me the opportunity to do both.

Working with you on all manner of city building activities has been one of the greatest highlights of my life.

Aside from my family, there is nothing for me more personally gratifying than working with other citizens in our community to address a civic challenge or identify an opportunity we can make happen together. I feel very lucky to have found in Toronto a place where so many others felt the same way.

When I moved to Toronto nearly thirty years ago, I am embarrassed to say that I did not really know very much about the city. It did not take long for me to become charmed by the wonderful diversity of the city's neighbourhoods and people, the green spaces in our unique ravines and along the lake, and dozens of other surprises, both large and small.

But the most amazing thing that struck me at every turn was how many people from all walks of life in this city were passionately concerned with making it a great city. There was a wide belief that Toronto had something special to offer the world. There was deep pride in big things the city had done — like building a great transit system — and equal passion for how to get the small things right, like making our neighbourhoods truly successful.

I also discovered that Toronto is a uniquely open city in the sense that people here cross boundaries more easily than in other places — no doubt partly due to the fact we have so many immigrants from so many different cultures. That openness made it easy to connect with others on civic projects. For me, the largest of these has been working with so many of you on the Toronto City Summit Alliance (TCSA).

November 2009 marked the seventh anniversary of the launch of the TCSA.

At last count there have been over six thousand volunteers involved in Alliance activities. Some of these are working on large current projects such as DiverseCity (partnered with Maytree), or Greening Greater Toronto — both of which came out of our 2007 Summit. Others have contributed to smaller and more informal activities. The work of the Alliance these past seven years has rested firmly on the many contributions of these volunteers drawn from all sectors of civil society.

Our Alliance CEO, Julia Deans, and our terrific staff have done a great job supporting all these activities, and on behalf of all involved in the TCSA I want to thank them for their hard work and incredible enthusiasm. I also want to thank all the organizations and individuals who have contributed financial and pro bono support. These contributions have made it possible to leverage the work of our volunteers dramatically.

As I look back at seven years of work at the TCSA, I think our founding principles in creating the Alliance have held up very well:

- Taking a regional perspective that recognizes many issues cross municipal boundaries.
- Tackling both the economic and social issues facing the region together. Toronto cannot be economically successful without having a strong social infrastructure that addresses education, poverty, the integration of immigrants, the strength of our neighbourhoods, and other fundamental social needs.
- Convening all sectors of civil society around the same table with leaders from the business community, the non-profit sectors, labour, and government.
- Being strictly non-partisan in all we do.
- Staying open and welcoming to anyone who was interested in getting involved.
- Committing to action, or as someone on our steering committee said, "no reports just sitting on the shelf."

As the Alliance has worked with partners across the region, it has been gratifying this past year to see continued developments on some of the remaining areas that we focused on in our original action plan, "Enough Talk." Metrolinx, for example, is now up and running and starting to tackle the regional transportation issues facing us.

It is also very gratifying to see the Ontario Child Benefit, the Federal Working Income Tax Benefit, and other ideas that so many of you contributed to during the MISWAA project now being funded by the province and the federal government and making such a significant difference in the lives of low income families in our region and across the rest of Ontario and the country. It is a good example of the power of all sectors working together to address a very complex set of issues and finding a consensus that could move things forward. There is still much in the MISWAA report and the work of others that needs to be done, but these initial steps by governments have already made a great difference.

It has also been exciting this year to see groups like the Emerging Leaders Network spawning a whole new generation of creative and social initiatives, and in the process stimulating connections across communities and sectors that have not been connected before.

Like so many aspects of city building, as people work on projects outside their normal spheres of activity, they get connected to new people and sectors in the city, and the power and value of everything gets multiplied many times over.

There will be a lot of discussion next year about Toronto's future. The election of new political leaders — mayors and councillors — will be important for all our municipal governments. But of equally profound importance is a broader question: "What really is our collective vision for Toronto — this city region five million of us call home?" Often when that question is posed, the response is likely to be a long list of attributes describing what Toronto should or could be. And sometimes, such discussions descend into negative territory: what doesn't work in Toronto, why so many issues seem stuck in gridlock, or worst of all, why we so often seem to lack the resources to enable important new ideas to happen.

Perhaps we are responding to the question the wrong way. I believe that good ideas and civic projects with a strong consensus and collective support will attract resources. We have seen this happen with the campaign to build or renovate seven major new cultural buildings across the city. Regarded by many as "too much at once" and "impossible to fund," these ambitious projects are succeeding because of the great work done up-front to build the consensus, plan and commission the facilities, and coordinate the fundraising.

As I look at the future of Toronto, I am as excited as I have ever been about what the 5 million people here have to offer the world. To me the potential of Toronto lies not so much within its architectural or economic or social possibilities as in what it could represent to the world as a place where amazing things get done because this city is full of conveners, of civic entrepreneurs, of people who understand in their collective DNA how to bring all the parts of civil society around a table to solve problems, seize opportunities, and make great things happen.

It is this capacity of social mobilization that can be Toronto's greatest gift to the world. We should stop worrying about global rankings and focus on what will make us truly special — which is that we can be the best in the world at collective leadership.

We can be a city where collective leadership is the norm. A city where civic entrepreneurs are everywhere and the process of bringing all the parts of civil society together to solve a problem is really how the city defines its uniqueness. A city where this quality is the essence of what makes Toronto so special.

In that sense, Toronto's gift to the world could be this unique and powerful model of city building that comes from collective leadership.

A city that is filled with civic entrepreneurs practicing collective leadership will be able to face any challenge and do all kinds of great things on economic issues, social issues, education, the arts, the environment, leveraging the richness of our diversity, and much much more.

When I look back at the all the civic projects that we have had the chance to work on, I am filled with huge appreciation for all that we have done together. When the Toronto City Summit Alliance launched in 2002, it could start quickly, because it stood on an incredible foundation of work across many years and many sectors by passionate city-builders who came before. Toronto is lucky to have so many people who care so much about making this a truly great city.

I want to take this opportunity to thank you for all that we have shared and done together and your support on so many civic initiatives. Now is a good time for us to pause, reflect upon, and celebrate that collective city building.

Thank you for all your enthusiasm, your trust and, most importantly, your passion for working together to realize the full potential of our great city.

David Pecaut

December 2009

OF RELATED INTEREST

Eugene Forsey, Canada's Maverick Sage
by Helen Forsey
978-1926577159
$35.00

Feisty and erudite, Eugene Alfred Forsey (1904–1991) was an activist scholar, labour researcher, constitutional expert, and senator who fought all his life for the common good. His speeches, articles, and letters informed and provoked Canadians for more than sixty years, and now his daughter brings that legacy back to life in this fascinating and relevant book. One of Canada's foremost constitutional experts, Forsey was also a provocative voice for social justice. Legendary for his sharp wit and high principle, he brought encyclopedic knowledge, irascible tenacity, and common sense to the causes of democracy, justice, and equality for all. Those themes resound through this book and provide a rich resource for Canadians facing the challenges of the twenty-first century.

Writing History
A Professor's Life
by Michael Bliss
978-1554889532
$40.00

One of Canada's best-known and most-honoured biographers turns to the raw material of his own life in *Writing History*. A university professor, prolific scholar, public intellectual, and frank critic of the world he has known, Michael Bliss draws on extensive personal diaries to describe a life that has taken him from small-town Ontario in the 1950s to international recognition for his books in Canadian and medical history. His memoir ranges remarkably widely: it encompasses social history, family tragedy, a critical insider's view of university life, Canadian national politics, and, above all, a rare glimpse into the craftsmanship that goes into the research and writing of history in our time.

 **DUNDURN**
www.dundurn.com

Visit us at
Dundurn.com
Definingcanada.ca
@dundurnpress
Facebook.com/dundurnpress